Ignite All

Ignite All

Leadership, Team Enablement, & Sparking That Inner Flame

The Fusion Team

BEP

BUSINESS EXPERT PRESS

Leader in applied, concise business books

First published in 2024 by
Business Expert Press, LLC
222 East 46th Street, New York, NY 10017
www.businessexpertpress.com

ISBN-13: 978-1-63742-614-2 (paperback)
ISBN-13: 978-1-63742-615-9 (e-book)

Business Expert Press Human Resource Management and Organizational Behavior Collection

First edition: 2024

10 9 8 7 6 5 4 3 2 1

*To those who bring their whole selves to their teams and those
finding their path*

Description

Putting a team together is easy. Creating a dynamic team culture is hard. Fusion brings a new world approach to leadership, team enablement, and sparking that inner flame. In this book—written by a team, for teams—**Fusion** distills proven best practices, methodologies, and frameworks that drive impactful change for small and large teams in the corporate workplace by incorporating models to build thoughtful processes, form empathetic teams, and develop team members into changemakers.

- **Unleash your talent:** Build a top-performing team utilizing proven best practices that activate your team's greatest assets.
- **Supercharge your team:** Level up your game with innovative methodologies and systems that shift your mindset and accelerate your team.
- **Amplify your impact:** Bring even greater value to the universe while keeping inclusion and diversity at the forefront.

Keywords

leadership development strategies; dynamic team culture enhancement; strategies for team collaboration; effective employee engagement techniques; techniques for talent development; strategies for employee motivation; frameworks for organizational resilience; methodologies for change management; models for team cohesion; continuous innovation methods; practices for psychological safety; strategies for building high-performance teams; techniques for creative problem-solving; approaches to performance feedback; strategies for maintaining work-life balance

Contents

Chapter Overview

Part 1: Unstoppable Talent

Chapter 1: Purpose, Passion, People

Great teams are comprised of individuals who overcome obstacles as a unit and commit hearts and minds to a common mission.

Chapter 2: Unlocking Communication

By understanding how people see the world, we can better communicate our intentions and operate from a position of empathy.

Chapter 3: Inclusion and Diversity

The foundation of an elite team starts with building an inclusive environment that will allow diverse teams to thrive.

Chapter 4: Virtuous Cycles

Creating a repeatable positive pattern where one good event leads to another, feeding on itself to make continuous improvement.

Chapter 5: Stay Curious

The ability to ask better questions and learn answers faster dramatically increases the frequency and speed of value delivery.

Chapter 6: Artists and Scientists

Perfecting your workflow for maximum output to produce your best work.

Part 2: Empowering Teams

Chapter 7: Intentional Communication

Daily, weekly, and monthly rituals will deeply connect a team when they foster psychological safety and transparency.

Chapter 8: Value Blueprinting

Building a thoughtful approach to your systems and their evolutions in a way that directly reflects your team's values.

Chapter 9: Elite Team Structure

Choosing to be a team in identity, structure, and achievement creates a magnification of positive impact and opportunity.

Chapter 10: Team System

Through intentional team system design, you can maximize your team's results while growing as individuals.

Chapter 11: Team Growth and Expansion

By maximizing investment in new hires at the start of their roles, you can enhance their experience, performance, and achievement.

Part 3: Creating Massive Value

Chapter 12: Creating Massive Value

Balancing the two forces of self-interest and caring for others helps you create massive value for all.

Chapter 13: Value-Based Marketing System

Building marketing systems based on the value you provide to your customers enables a zero-lift ecosystem of content creation, communication, and brand equity.

Chapter 14: Enabling People, Organizations, the World

By leading with empathy and a no-fear mindset, teams can activate change-making energy in people across the world.

Chapter 15: Creating Conscious Connections

Aligning passions and investing skills in high-impact non-profits builds ecosystems that can change the world.

Chapter 16: Outrageous Leadership

Our job as leaders is to have people realize and activate their greatest capabilities.

Introduction

By Ed Boudrot, VP, Fusion

This book is for those who are trying to change the world and make an impact on the greater good. No matter whether you work in a company or run your own, we hope you create a beautiful environment and experience for the people around you.

Focus on Your Community . . .

We want you to create virtuous cycles where one good thing leads to another, creating continuous excitement and improvement. We want you to think about the experience of new employees and those currently in your organization shaping its future. We want you to embrace eclectic passions, understand people at the deepest level—what they love—and drive and enhance those passions. We want you to think about the massive value that you are creating for others around the world and those in your immediate circle. We want you to consciously make connections with your community by investing your core skills in others, creating value, and growing a worldwide network for good.

Focus on Your Team . . .

We want you to create teams of passionate, purpose-driven people committed to a common mission. We want you to be an exceptional leader by leveraging inclusion and diversity because it's all around us. We want you to create an inclusive and safer space. We want you to think of yourself and the teams around you as artists and scientists perfecting workflow and output. We want you to reflect on the impact of precision communication and how to run your team effectively, fully understanding your goals and objectives and balancing them with a deep care for one another. We want you to create a blueprint of your unique and differentiated business operations to incrementally improve 1 percent a day toward meaningful outcomes. We want you to think about an elite team structure that is unparalleled in creating a positive impact. We want you to prioritize your brand as a vehicle for teaching and value creation to set the tone of who you are and what you stand for as a team.

Focus on Yourself . . .

We want you to be unstoppable. We want you to embrace your eclectic passions. We want you to stay curious and develop systems to build your efficiency and value delivery. We want you to be the player, the coach, and the team leader who prioritizes the growth of others. And, finally, we want you to be the selfless leader who focuses on serving others.

PART 1

Unstoppable Talent

Start With a Match

By Lianza Reyes

its head unassuming, appearing fragile
wondering if using it is even worthwhile
give it a chance and strike it against a surface,
and now you marvel at its expanse of purpose
that's the possibility of any one person,
and the right opportunity to become their best version.
give them the right moments, and they never stop
they show their multitudes and do more than a great job
minds working in tandem, the seeds blooming flowers,
couldn't stop them if you wanted, now that they hold their power
to each their own, and their own becomes *ours*
if we play to our strengths with a similar cause,
through all this, you see what you can make happen
when everyone has a chance to show *unstoppable talent.*

CHAPTER 1

Purpose, Passion, People

By Colby Champagne

There is a formula that will change the way you work. Each ingredient must exist in harmony with the others. Quantities can change, what's important is, the quality of ingredients, and how they combine. Changing proportions will change the result. It just depends on what you need at a particular moment in time and in your career.

A Simple Recipe: Purpose, Passion, and People

Purpose means being an integral part of a system, fighting to make an impact on the world. Passion builds a connection to our work and the pride we feel knowing that we are creating a new future for our consumers. People stand alongside one another to make it happen. These ingredients create an elite enterprise team.

Ingredient #1: Purpose

Humans crave purpose. A team that feels connected to their work and their impact will experience greater retention and results. This ingredient should be ubiquitous across all aspects of your team, and it is critical for the formula to work properly.

Connection to Meaningful Work Drives Satisfaction

A virtuous cycle is "a chain of events in which one desirable occurrence leads to another which further promotes the first occurrence and so on."[1] Consider this cycle in relation to the employee experience. Happy employees are more likely to deliver exceptional work which creates financial returns. Meaningful work contributes to employee happiness. *Harvard Business Review* reports that over 90 percent of employees would trade a percentage of their lifetime earnings if guaranteed that their work would always be meaningful.[2] At the annual Massachusetts Conference for Women, where over 10,000 attendees gathered, individuals were asked to choose between a hypothetical raise and a boss who prioritized them finding meaning in work. It turned out that 80 percent of attendees reported that they would forego a 20 percent raise in favor of a boss invested in their pursuit to find fulfilling work.[3] The workforce is clearly craving authentic connection to their work. Employee engagement is just one piece of the virtuous cycle. Research shows that high levels of job satisfaction are inversely correlated with absenteeism and employee churn and positively correlated with work drive, morale, and productivity.[4] An engaged workforce shows up, spreads joy, and produces quality work, leading to tangible business results. Four years ago, I attended an innovation conference and met our team, Fusion, for the first time. I was attracted to their human-centered approach to problem-solving and their laser focus on their broader mission to help people live healthier lives. I saw a life-size persona named Linda and launched into conversation with the team about Linda's greatest challenges and life goals. I eagerly asked how they built a new product to resolve her pain points. Fast forward to today, and my experience acts as a case study for why purpose is so important: I feel connected to my work and team, which inspires me to challenge myself and over-deliver quality results, which in turn feeds creative strategies and incredible products. Telling you to engage and inspire your team is easy. Showing you how is more complex—and we are up for the challenge.

Demonstrate How Your Team Adds Value From the Start

When I say, "from the start," I mean before Day 1: in the interview process. When I polled my teammates about the moment they each realized Fusion was different from other teams, many mentioned their interviews. The presence of the team during the interview said more about our culture, collaboration style, and project work than any job description. We find that behavioral and case-based interviews do not create an interview experience representative of who we are as a team or the types of high-impact projects we get to tackle. Instead, we designed an interview experience in which we invite interviewees to "work with us for a day," and they partner with us to problem-solve an anonymized project we have completed in the past. By demonstrating the nature of our work and its connection to our broader mission, applicants can evaluate us and our work for a potential fit while we evaluate them. Our interview approach shows that we are invested in our applicants' success before they even receive an offer, and it gives a firsthand look into our meaningful projects. We want high-performing teammates who feel connected to our work and our greater purpose.

Connect to Meaningful Work From Day 1

Reflect on the last time you joined a new team. Your first few weeks were filled with administrative requirements, introductions, and some light-weight work before fully diving into your new responsibilities. This is the experience we expect, but it is not the experience we deserve. Our team believes the welcoming experience should be a quick ramp and action-packed. We balance that expectation with the support necessary to be and feel successful right away.

- Framework download: Spend an hour daily learning and applying the core Fusion frameworks with their onboarding Launchpad (more about the Launchpad in Chapter 11, "Team Growth and Expansion").
- Keepers and Improvers: Provide candid feedback at the end of each day using a simple framework of Keepers and Improvers[4]—what went well and what could be improved.
- Schedule and lead team one-on-ones: Take time to meet with each team member for introductions, asking one consistent question of each existing team member, like "What keeps you excited to come to work?" or "What is your superpower on the team?" (more on superpowers later).

- Support an engagement: If a new hire joins the team during a major project milestone, they will take on a support role. Our record is a new hire jumping in on Day 2! This demonstrates our trust in their skillset and provides immediate exposure to our work.

Regardless of whether a new teammate is a seasoned professional with 25 years of experience or a recent college grad, everybody is expected and encouraged to contribute on their first day. We treat one another as equals regardless of role or title, and we demonstrate this as soon as someone joins the team.

> **Reflect:** What part of your onboarding process can you change to empower new hires to add value from Day 1?

Ingredient #2: Passion

Passion fuels behavior. Emotional connections between your team and their work create loyalty and engagement. You can catalyze those emotional connections through intentional design and execution of your team's culture.

A Team's Culture Should Be a Carefully Crafted Reflection of the Individuals Who Comprise It

Systems thinking is a widely coveted skill among great leaders. It is the ability to apply a macro lens when problem-solving. Good systems thinkers can abstract upstream to spot patterns and zoom downstream to understand nuances in the way processes within a system interact. Excellent systems thinkers proactively identify opportunities to flip the system on its head. They incorporate their passion and values into their work to intentionally alter those systems in pursuit of a cause. Ruth Bader Ginsberg's dissenting opinions embody impassioned systems thinking. She says "Dissents speak to a future age . . . The greatest dissents do become court opinions and gradually over time their views become the dominant view. So that's the dissenter's hope: that they are writing not for today, but for tomorrow." RBG dissented for the downstream, longer-term effects. In the context of team performance and how we work together, a systems thinker appreciates that upstream actions comprising team culture (spoken and unspoken, visible and invisible rituals) have a massive downstream impact (engagement levels, collaboration styles, and overall satisfaction at work). Each discrete action we take sends a message about our values both within and outside our organization. To create a healthy culture and attract talent, we must recognize that everything we do—both unspoken and explicit norms—either reinforces our values or works against them. Our responsibility is to understand what excites, interests, and drives teammates forward, then actively create changes in our systems to reflect that.

Understand Your Team's "Personal Whys"

Simon Sinek is an author, speaker, thought leader, and "an unshakable optimist." His work implores individuals to start with *why*. In his 2009 TedTalk "How great leaders inspire action," his mic-drop moment is when he declares "People don't buy what you do, they buy why you do it."[5] He exposes the simple reason why some succeed while others fail at seemingly the same thing. *Why* someone endeavors to do something matters more than *what* they do. The *why* builds community, connection, and understanding among people. Sinek has been one of the most influential thought leaders in the development of our team's culture. The *why* concept can be applied with an introspective lens. First, we must understand our own *why*—the personal mission that guides our career and life decisions. Then, we can find meaning in the value we deliver as individuals and as part of a team. Demonstrating our commitment to everyone's *why* and the team's *why* is critical to fostering a purposeful culture. Fusion's *why* was set by our founding team. It is our purpose for existing within the enterprise: to help others and positively impact every employee. The beautiful part is that each individual's *why* feeds into this collective one. Understanding, valuing, and supporting your team's personal *whys* creates a purpose-driven and cohesive team. You must be intentional and inquire about, and follow up on your teams' *whys*. Actively connect team members with meaningful work and opportunities to grow in their areas of passion. This applies to both new and existing team members. For new team members, a personal *why* analysis should be part of onboarding. On our team, new teammates are paired with a dedicated onboarding mentor. The mentor navigates them through an experience called the Fusion Launchpad (more details in Chapter 11, "Team Growth and Expansion"). The Launchpad is a team-designed, interactive, web-based onboarding experience that supports new team members through their first few weeks. Aside from providing an overview of our team, culture, and favorite books, the Launchpad allows us to get to know our new team members. They will take time in their first few weeks to reflect on what they want to learn and set goals for the first 30, 60, and 90 days. They use this reflection to articulate their personal *why*, allowing us to make a conscious effort to connect them with meaningful work and like-minded mentors. For seasoned team members, the personal *why* should be an agenda topic at quarterly manager check-ins and yearly performance evaluations. It should be integrated into performance goals and deeply understood by managers and teammates alike, so individuals are empowered and supported in fulfilling their *why*.

Develop Your Cultural Guidelines

Your team is a unique group within a larger enterprise. You should have your own culture that represents your core values and what you seek to achieve. It should be distinct to your team and feed into the larger enterprise's culture. For example, here's how we've articulated our Fusion team values: no complaining; propose solutions; teach others; show up on time; beat deadlines; ask better questions; listen carefully; share credit; write "thank you" notes; take good notes; deliver quality work; be humble; measure results.

> **Reflect:** What keywords come to mind when you think about your team? How can you translate those into values?

Show—Don't Tell—Your Values

I interviewed a leader around corporate strategy for inclusion and diversity, and they said: "If you are not inclusive, you have no business being diverse."

As a leader, you are responsible for embodying the values expected of your team. If you do not, no one will. We have our list of 13 team principles reflecting our values alongside unspoken expectations that are an innate part of how we operate and who we are as a team. One example is, "never cancel one-on-ones." A combination of listen carefully, show up on time, and be humble, we understand that demonstrating our commitment to one another takes priority over 30 minutes of deep work. Reschedule, but never cancel a one-on-one. Another example is intentionally rotating who leads internal meetings. Rotating combines our principles of teach others, share credit, and be humble. This ritual gives every team member the opportunity to practice leading, and we all benefit from observing diverse leadership styles. Reflect on the nuances of your team operations and consider how to create moments for everyone on your team to embody your team values.

Share the Knowledge

Everyone benefits when we are a more informed team. My team's shared values demonstrate that our desire for transparency and symmetric information transcends all 13 values. We designed them to ensure our behavior encourages knowledge share.

A siloed team duplicates work, misses deadlines, and produces mediocre results. When teams are communicative about project context, status updates, and learnings, they are more effective, efficient, and exceed expectations. Seamless communication and knowledge sharing give teams insight into the bigger picture and allow team members to understand their upstream and downstream impact. This transparency and visibility further connection to the work and the mission. Consider implementing some of the following best practices from Table 1.1.

These practices have contributed to our transparent and learning-focused team culture, a reflection of the respect and support we have for one another. It creates space to explore our passions and learn more about new ones.

Ingredient #3: People

Purpose and passion equate to very little without the right people behind them.

Table 1.1 Fusion's operational best practices

Subject	Why	How	What
Team Capacity	Understand who to tap for a new project, who to ask for ad hoc support, and who is uninterruptable	Team-wide round-robin of each person's priorities, their level of urgency, and what that individual's capacity is that week	30-minute weekly focused standup
Project Updates*	Provide a big-picture perspective of the varied work the team is doing	Introduce new projects, discuss recent intake calls, and provide updates on existing work (consider a digital task management system like Trello)	30-minute weekly focused standup
Strategy Insights	See around corners by drawing connec-tions and sensing patterns across client work	Create a consistent structure for each project lead to use to review mis-sion-critical insights from recent engagements	Event-driven (e.g., after wrapping an engagement)
Retrospec-tive	Commit to continu-ous improvement by sharing engagement highs and lows	Present greatest learnings and best practices from a tactical, execution perspective	Event-driven (e.g., after wrapping an engagement)

*Create an objective framework for why and how decisions are made regarding new work. Share it with your team and empower emerging leaders to apply it.

Above All, Work Should Be Human

Focus on Connection, Set Work-Life Boundaries, and Foster Professional Growth.

The COVID-19 pandemic changed the way we seek connection at work and in our personal lives. Today, much of the corporate workforce remains remote. Leaders worldwide continue to offer perspectives on the future of at-home versus in-office work. We must prepare for any future, whether remote, in-person, or hybrid. With that in mind, we must foreground the third ingredient of the elite enterprise team: Peo-ple. Prior to the pandemic, we made a conscious shift to be excellent at virtual collaboration. We were constantly solutioning for how to make our team—located at the time in Boston, MA and Raleigh, NC—a more inclusive place to work. We experimented with ways to make it feel like we were connected and equal across voices and cultures. We purchased high-quality microphones for our team rooms so each voice could be heard on virtual meetings. We maintained daily stand-up meetings across locations to encourage communication and breed transparency. Though nothing could have fully prepared us for March 2020, this work gave us a jump start. We are learning alongside the rest of the world how to create a virtual environment that maintains the chemistry that makes our team so special. We are committed to sharing what worked for us in the past and how we are evolving it to meet us where we are today.

Seek Meaningful Opportunities for Connection

In February 2020, our entire team traveled to Washington, D.C. for a 4-day early career national orientation. We were there to coach early career new hires around human-centered design through the lens of inclusion and team performance. We took advantage of this rare opportunity where all 18 of us were in one location. We planned outings around our work schedule—dinners, one-on-ones over coffee, team runs (or team ice cream runs for those less cardio-inclined)—anything to connect with other teammates. There is something special about spending time with colleagues outside of the office. It reminds me of how it felt when I was younger and would see a teacher outside of school. When we grow accustomed to seeing people in one environment, it is easy to forget that we have lives beyond work. Intentionally spending time together in these other environments builds a stronger, more connected, and supportive team. The key is to go beyond chatting over a drink. Activity-based outings have strengthened our interpersonal team connections and provided something to talk or joke about for weeks or years afterward. Consider volunteering, ice skating, or taking a cooking class instead of, or in addition to, your annual holiday party. If you are geographically dispersed, take advantage of moments when team members are in one place. Intentionally pair project leads from different sites. This gives them the opportunity to travel to the client location and spend time together inside and outside of work. We understand perfecting virtual collaboration is both a challenge and an immense opportunity. On our journey, we developed rituals to build connections whether dispersed or fully virtual. Weekly themed lunches bring teammates from all locations together for an engaging, nonwork-related discussion. Virtual trivia or game nights are always a hit (winner gets bragging rights). Level it up by having individuals teach the team something new—a Master Class in backpacking, pasta making, or car detailing. Challenge each other, learn from one another, and perhaps most importantly, have fun together. A little laughter can go a long way when it comes to connection.

Create a Workspace That Inspires Its People

In January 2020, we enlisted a pair of our talented designers in a top-secret endeavor: Secret Squirrel. It was a complete overhaul of our team's dedicated workspace. They invested hours on this project, applying their firsthand experience on the team and deep understanding of our needs to create an inspiring space. The term workspace is intentionally vague. Whether remote, in-person, or hybrid, we must stay true to our workspace principles. An effective workplace should inspire collaboration, communication, and creativity. Take a look at how each of these principles were applied to our physical space:

1. **Collaboration:** They increased working space by clearing furniture away from whiteboard walls. Sticky notes and markers were distributed throughout the room in clearly labeled carts.
2. **Communication:** They rearranged tables into a U-shape to encourage visual connection during team meetings. They purchased additional microphones around the room to improve audio for calls.
3. **Creativity:** They styled the room with artifacts from our recently launched brand refresh (with plenty of snacks!).

In March 2020 we had to completely rethink the way we collaborated as a team when we all shifted to mandatory remote work. We reconsidered our tools, the nature and frequency of meetings and team norms:

1. **Collaboration:** We transitioned to a virtual whiteboard that enabled us to work together internally and with clients. We also switched to a communication platform that enabled real-time document editing amongst project groups.

2. **Communication:** When in meetings, we keep our videos on and the chat box active. In our collaboration platform, channels vary from project work to interesting articles to photos of pets or favorite recipes. It is also a norm to call a teammate for an impromptu virtual desk drop-by or project consultation.

3. **Creativity:** Team members are encouraged to research and experiment with new virtual tools. We share our findings to expand and strengthen our team's capacity to continuously adapt.

Value and Celebrate Individuals

It is important to develop rituals of recognition and celebration, so the team feels valued and seen. Though it may not be the only reason we are driven to exceed expectations, recognition for our work reinforces our individual impact. Recognition can come in many forms and from anyone on the team:

- A casual one-on-one message expressing congratulations
- A text from your manager or mentor expressing gratitude
- A team-wide e-mail or message highlighting an individual or project team's hard work or excellent client feedback
- A summary of the week's incredible accomplishments e-mailed to your leadership chain
- A thoughtful gift or outing to celebrate a birthday, work anniversary, or personal accomplishment

Regardless of its format, recognition and celebration feel good. It keeps us connected to one another, to our work, and to our team.

Know Your Superpowers

We love a *good* icebreaker that challenges us to reflect, warm up our minds, and inspire creativity. A *good* icebreaker adds depth to human connection. One of our favorites is "What is your superpower?" Knowing the unique value that individuals bring allows us to better understand, develop, and connect with one another. My superpower is problem-solving with a hyper-focus on the consumer. I challenge myself and those around me to think and feel what our consumers might think and feel. These superpowers can be leveraged in the following scenarios:

1. **Recruiting:** Based on your knowledge of team members' superpowers, recruit what is missing. Ask the applicant about their superpower and evaluate how it could complement the team.
2. **Onboarding:** Welcome a new hire with superpower introductions. The team learns something about their new teammate, and the new hire can more quickly understand who to seek for help, mentorship, or an interesting chat.

> **Reflect:** What is your superpower? How does it complement your direct reports, peers, and leaders?

We Are Human

We are parents, siblings, caregivers, and individuals. We have responsibilities, hobbies, and passions that extend far beyond our forty-plus hours together each week. But it is easy to forget about what makes us human when we are distracted by the whirlwind of work. We pride ourselves in being a team grounded in empathy, which we must apply to—and demonstrate in—everything we do. This includes how we approach one another and our respective ecosystems: take care of yourself first, family second, and work third. We have felt the great sadness a beloved teammate experienced as she supported her mother through a cancer diagnosis and end of life. We gave her the space and flexibility she needed to work when and where was best for her. We experienced the stress of a mother trying to balance supporting her young kids' remote learning schedule with her work responsibilities. We were able to arrange a part-time schedule that allowed her to continue working with us and spend more time with her kids. We supported a new father as he adjusted his working hours to complement his wife's night shifts so their young daughter could have more "mommy and daddy" time and less time at daycare. A mental health day, flexibility to care for a loved one, or a short walk to clear your mind can all positively influence the quality and efficacy of your work and increase personal satisfaction.

> **Reflect:** How might your team build in greater empathy and compassion for one another?

Key Takeaways

Purpose: Focus on the Why

Teams with a clearly defined purpose and a shared passion can do anything. Schedule an hour with your team to crowdsource your team's *why* and share your personal *whys*. Draw a connection to each *why* in everything you do, creating a framework to evaluate new projects against these *whys*. Articulate how they relate to your organization's *why*.

Passion: Build an Intentional Culture

Develop a culture that empowers team members to live their values and evolve it over time. Write down a list of your team rituals. Audit the list to ensure they promote your values. If they do, intentionally and consistently integrate those rituals into your team's operations. If they do not, create new ones.

People: Connect on a Personal Level

Get to know your team beyond their work. Schedule a quarterly all-team meeting and assign a rotating team lead to design an agenda. Focus the agenda on learning, trying new experiences, or having fun together.

CHAPTER 2

Unlocking Communication

By Jeremy Smith

Our team is constantly on the hunt for tools and methods to perfect our craft, hone our processes, and create new possibilities with our existing skills. It seems that "new" innovations often result from a small shift in perspective or approach. This chapter explores team communication and how it can be enlightened through the lens of the Enneagram. Understanding the behavior of ourselves and our teammates can help us decipher words and actions into the core intention.

Many systems exist to categorize personality traits and define how individuals process information, make decisions, and get motivated. The Myers-Briggs Type Indicator (MBTI) is an industry standard in counseling, business, and education industries. It focuses on how individuals perceive and process information but doesn't explore why they operate that way. The Big Five system is scientifically validated and measures five key traits. It is a great tool for individual personality assessments but is not easily applicable to communication and relationships. DISC is another scientifically validated model that categorizes an individual's behavioral expression of emotions. However, the DISC model does not delve into thoughts and motivations. The Clifton Strengths assessment identifies the things you are good at and how to maximize your potential. It's a great tool for honing your strengths but does not address personality traits that may be negatively impacting your work or relationships.

The Enneagram in Figure 2.1 contains nine basic personality types, and each person has a core personality type. Most people adopt some

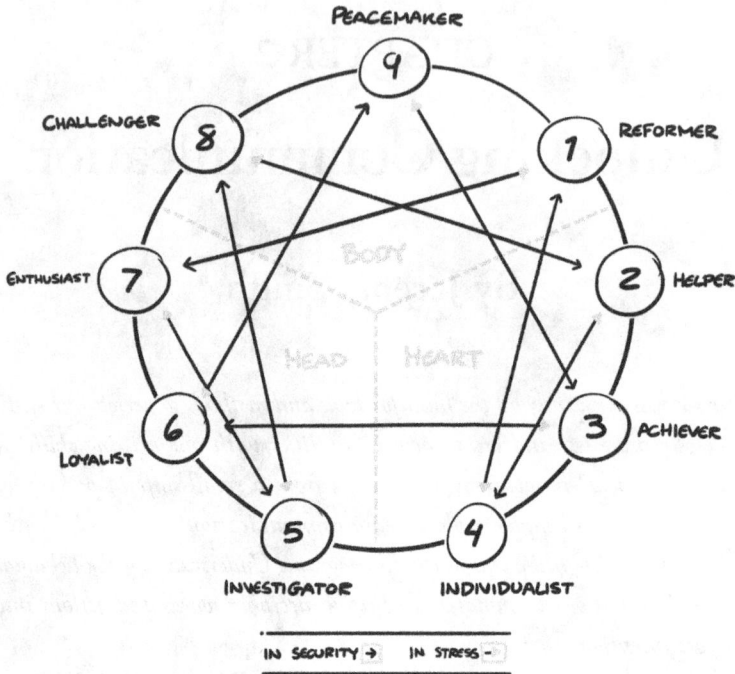

Figure 2.1 The Enneagram

The Enneagram is a system for understanding how people interpret the world and the motivations behind their behavior.

traits from a wing or sibling type. The nine types are categorized within one of three centers of intelligence—body, heart, and head. These are how we engage the world. The Body triad emphasizes action, the Heart triad is dominated by feelings, and the Head triad prioritizes thinking. All humans operate across these three centers, and our shift into centers beyond our core is driven by motivation or fear, health or unhealth. Although our core number becomes fixed between late adolescence to early adulthood, security or stress can shift our behavior toward other numbers. Both external and internal events can influence our movement between healthy, average, and low average ranges of behavior. First, learn about yourself, then adopt a position of grace with your teammates.

While there are some quick and helpful learnings from the Enneagram, there are also some limitations to the system. It is a self-reported system without robust scientific research or studies supporting which classification applies to an individual, so its results can be subjective. The

Enneagram is also quite revealing and requires team members to share aspects of themselves that may be embarrassing or uncomfortable. We often present ourselves differently at work than in other life scenarios. Reasons for this range from needing to fulfill a role to masking a side of ourselves perceived as weak or unhelpful in the workplace. The beauty of the Enneagram lies in the fact that all of us have the strengths and perspectives our team needs. A sense of belonging, psychological safety, and trust within the team are key in enabling us to understand and exercise those strengths to evolve communication.

We don't have space to fully unwrap all aspects of the Enneagram, but there are resources at the end of the chapter. Each of us is on a journey of self-understanding—wherever you find yourself, the Enneagram can offer insight into the motivations for behavior triggers that influence your thoughts and actions. Understanding this about yourself is freeing, and better understanding your colleagues can be life changing.

Type One

Ones have been referred to as perfectionists and reformers. These labels are driven by the One's need for things to be done "right" and their desire for justice and fairness. They have an inner voice grading every action and this voice comments on both their own actions and thoughts and those of the world around them. When they feel there is a right way to do something, they will pursue that course of action with a deliberate intensity that is driven by rational decisions—sometimes to the point of redirecting or turning off emotion so as not to negatively affect achieving the goal.

When secure, Ones adopt characteristics from Seven.

Ones have decisive opinions on what is right and wrong and can be strong advocates in defending the rights of others. Healthy Ones have an optimistic worldview and allow themselves to relax their drive for perfection, becoming more spontaneous and playful. They feel empowered to take appropriate actions resulting in positive outcomes for others. Their attention to detail and penchant for action allows them to make rapid progress in their endeavors, making them reliable team members.

When stressed, Ones adopt characteristics from Four.

Ones strive to be virtuous. While this is good, under stress it can result in Ones being overly critical of themselves and others, struggling to receive criticism. This internal struggle with "imperfection" can lead to anger, which they will try to contain but others will see it leak out through nonverbal behavior.

How to relate: Be clear about what you need a One to own so that they don't get trapped trying to handle everything. Help them to know when something is done well enough so that they can move on. Be honest and gentle with criticism or conflict. Show Ones that you appreciate their effort and tell them that they are good.

Type Two

Relationship is a core factor in a *Two*'s life. They find personal value in meeting the needs of others and excel at helping others feel valued and included. Their natural empathy for others helps Twos build connections and makes them great at meeting new people and working in a team. Twos typically know a lot of people and are proactive about maintaining the relationship. They understand and can feel others' feelings.

When secure, Twos adopt characteristics from Four.

A healthy Two is a pleasure to be around. They're fun, caring, and generous. They notice the needs of those around them and are accepting and inclusive. Twos love to be helpful, and foster relationships with everyone they meet. When a Two is in tune with themselves, they can acknowledge their intrinsic self-worth separated from a connection with someone else. This ability to recognize their value frees them up to offer even more genuine love and caring for others.

When stressed, Twos adopt characteristics from Eight.

Twos find great pleasure and purpose in meeting others' needs; however, this can cause Twos to overextend themselves. If this happens, they might feel underappreciated and adopt controlling behaviors, or they may doubt their value (being unable to give more) and retreat from the relationship.

How to relate: Conversation with a Two is easy—they love talking with anybody. Keep it casual and avoid filling it with everything you need from them. Twos can elicit too much self-worth from meeting others' needs while ignoring or denying their own needs. Be gentle and clear with conflict and feedback. Show appreciation for their hard work, and that you value them outside of anything they do for you.

Type Three

Threes excel at reading an audience and determining exactly what is needed to deliver success. Threes love goals and winning, which merges nicely with their honesty, integrity, and care for others. They can be great leaders and employees as they strive to bring value and admiration to themselves and their team.

When secure, Threes adopt characteristics from Six.

If there are new relationships to be made, a Three is the perfect person for the job. They thrive on reading people and finding synergies in their connections, being able to modify their approach to meet the needs of the engagement. New challenges excite them, and they enjoy planning a path to success. Threes can tap into the energy of competition and use it to drive them toward their goal. They appreciate both personal and professional challenges, so offer opportunities that support their personal growth.

When stressed, Threes adopt characteristics from Nine.

Being goal-oriented, Threes can tie their personal worth to success. If they were unable to meet a goal, they have a hard time accepting praise or attention. Threes can get so focused on achieving a goal that they work too hard and are unable to relate to others, consumed in a persona they've adopted to accomplish the goal.

How to relate: Threes are optimistic, so don't overload them with negativity. Be upfront and clear about what you need from them—they want to help you but might not know how. They need to hear praise and approval, so be generous with words of affirmation. Threes want concise, constructive criticism, seeing it as an opportunity to improve.

Type Four

People who are creative, original, and expressive are often *Fours*. They crave authenticity, are very emotive, and want to be understood. They see beyond the surface level of a situation, tapping into emotional drivers and highlighting the possibilities of what could be. Energy and optimism fuel their passion and heart for service while staying tuned in to the context and needs of others. They can embrace the complexity of both beauty and struggle.

When secure, Fours adopt characteristics from One.

Fours have no fear or aversion to intense emotion and can be extremely empathetic toward others. They see beauty in emotions that others may suppress, and this enables them to care for, respect, and support others through emotional encounters. Fours love deeply and embrace opportunities for personal growth, placing high value on relationships built on authenticity. Their aptitude for beauty allows them to translate intent and purpose into a pleasing aesthetic presentation.

When stressed, Fours adopt characteristics from Two.

Fours can romanticize what was or what could be. This "ideal" image can cause them to focus on what is missing. When deficiency takes center stage, it can lead Fours to withdraw from tough situations or turn inward, viewing the inadequacy as rooted in themselves.

How to relate: Fours appreciate the authentic dialogue that includes emotional honesty. Give them space to do their work and freedom to utilize their creativity. If they seem melancholic, model a steady presence, and avoid telling them to "snap out of it." If their mood dynamics are affecting you, be honest and let them know because they care about you. If a Four is feeling down on themselves, acknowledge their feelings and remind them of their values.

Type Five

Fives are attuned to investigation and observation. They don't react with emotion and remain neutral in their position and when processing information. When a Five comes across a topic of interest or needs to find a solution, they will dive deep into learning all they can about the subject. When they are done investigating, they will achieve an advanced understanding of the topic; however, they can also get lost in discovery and fail to do anything with their knowledge. Fives also tend to have strict relational boundaries to support their need for introspection, allowing them to be trustworthy and respectful of the boundaries of others.

When secure, Fives adopt characteristics from Eight.

Healthy Fives are a valuable asset for any team or relationship as they will use their investigatory skills to find the best path forward and then explain that position with clarity and authority. While they may see social engagements as draining, their interactions are engaged, sincere, and attentive to those with whom they interact. They typically keep a limited number of close relationships but are often generous and considerate in those relationships.

When stressed, Fives adopt characteristics from Seven.

Fives typically bypass emotion on their way to analyzing a situation. Thinking brings them comfort and they must be intentional to consider emotions—of their own and others. When Fives feel drained by social interaction, they can present as unempathetic or cold. They can be overly self-reliant and miss out on the benefits of engaging with and learning from those around them.

How to relate: If you need to discuss something important with a Five, give them a heads up on the topic so they can process their thoughts before the conversation. Be straightforward and honest in your interactions, opting for a logical rather than emotional approach. Fives like to know exactly what is expected of them and appreciate being valued for what they offer.

Type Six

Most of the organizations and groups we belong to benefit from the loyalty and commitment offered by *Sixes*. They care about their communities and enjoy building relationships. Sixes often see the world through a lens of what could go wrong, so they are naturally good at planning, problem-solving, and seeing things the rest of us might miss. Their attention to detail forms an ability to discern what lies beneath the surface, analyzing the complexities of people and situations.

When secure, Sixes adopt characteristics from Nine.

Sixes take a little time to build trust in relationships, but once they've decided you are trustworthy, they will be extremely faithful, supportive, and take care of you any way they can. Their determination and strength are a byproduct of their courage, and they will not put up with abuses of power by those in authority. Sixes care about the common good and seek ways to build community and structure that will support healthy outcomes for all.

When stressed, Sixes adopt characteristics from Three.

If someone is expressing a dominant opinion, Sixes may initially present an opposing view to test the validity of the dominant opinion. This helps them work through their aversion to easily accepting an opinion that they haven't been able to validate through data and logical analysis. Sixes seek stability and security in their relationships and when that is unavailable or taken from them, they can get lost in analyzing the situation, even to the point of projecting imagined reasons and scenarios onto others.

How to relate: Predictability is comforting for a Six, so schedule meetings with them and show up on time. Be honest and authentic; otherwise, it will dilute their trust in you. They are likely dealing with some anxiety, so allow them to share their concerns. Take those concerns seriously and then discuss the best possible outcomes. Remind them of when they successfully acted on their ideas, highlighting the good things they offer.

Type Seven

Sevens are the most optimistic people in our lives. Curiosity and spontaneity drive their explorations, and while it may make some people uncomfortable, we can't help but feel enlivened and hopeful when we tag along for the ride. The mind of a Seven is always "on" as they calculate opportunities, and their optimism allows them to see the best in people and situations. This positive vision empowers Sevens with a vivid imagination that capitalizes on their rapid thought and combination of various ideas and options.

When secure, Sevens adopt characteristics from Five.

With an eye on the future, Sevens can motivate people toward a common hope. They are generous and lighthearted; their ability to think and learn quickly allows them to pivot when needed. Sevens typically operate with a high level of energy, and this results in them being a source of invigoration for their friends and coworkers. Healthy Sevens can engage their discernment abilities, focus their mind, and drive toward specific outcomes with creativity and inspiration.

When stressed, Sevens adopt characteristics from One.

When situations get hectic, the Seven's ability to positively reframe everything can cause them to avoid negatives that must be resolved to progress. When they can't avoid coming face to face with painful emotions or situations, they can become overly critical or disengage as they move on to the next opportunity or adventure. Daily routine or long-term projects can be hard for Sevens as they thrive on variety. With their mind always on the lookout for new and exciting adventures, Sevens can be noncommittal—keeping their options open should a more interesting or engaging opportunity arise.

How to relate: Sevens feel constrained when presented with expectations, so frame conversations around their potential as opportunities and ask for their ideas. They don't like to dwell on or share emotions, so ask them to share stories to create space for their feelings. Structure conversations to be light and succinct and keep criticism short and sweet. Allow space for Sevens to voice their ideas because you'll both benefit, even if you go in a different direction. Allow the Seven's zeal for life to rub off on you and ask them to show you how to play again.

Type Eight

The simplest way to sum up *Eights* would be the word "action." Eights are the most energetic Enneagram type because they don't stop moving. They usually have very clear ideas on what needs to be done and they don't need a consensus to begin. Eights avoid weakness and vulnerability in themselves, and they'll be the first to jump in and protect anyone they see being abused or taken advantage of. They are committed to outcomes they believe in and support others along the journey. Eights are comfortable with confrontation. They will challenge anyone on any topic, using conflict to assess a situation, a person's conviction, or gauge trustworthiness.

When secure, Eights adopt characteristics from Two.

Eights are excellent team players who approach their work with all-in vigor. They enjoy getting a job done, can bring positive energy to the group, and are willing to step in and lead when needed. Eights provide clear communication and can envision the big picture, then distill it into immediate actions toward the goal. They do not shy away from chaotic scenarios, almost energized by the opportunities available in those situations. If an Eight views someone as under their care, they will advocate for them.

When stressed, Eights adopt characteristics from Five.

An extreme avoidance of real or perceived personal weakness can cause stressed Eights to be critical of themselves and those around them. Their default action when things go south is to work harder. This can worsen a situation when it might be better to pause and reconfigure action plans. With their focus on getting things done, Eights don't always see the value in relationship management and can be unaware of others' feelings.

How to relate: Eights respond best to direct, brief communication. Avoid centering a conversation on feelings or emotions because they don't trust that. Eights respect when someone stands up for their convictions, even if they disagree. They respect people who aren't pushovers, and if they have a problem with you, they will let you know. Eights prefer you directly discuss any issue you have with them rather than talking behind their back. They can handle it, and after a confrontation is over, they move on and don't think about it any longer.

Type Nine

Nines are peacemakers. They can see things from others' perspectives and mediate conflict from an honest, neutral position. Conflict is very discomforting for Nines so they seek to alleviate disputes around them. Their goal of harmony for the group is made evident in their inclusive support of everyone. They sometimes have trouble making decisions because there is less conflict in going along with others' preferences, and Nines generally don't have a strong opinion either way. However, if there is a serious decision to be made, Nines are quick and decisive with their opinion—which can surprise themselves and those around them.

When secure, Nines adopt characteristics from Three.

Since Nines are attentive to what is best for the group, they have an easier time speaking up and taking action when in a secure state, especially if there is injustice happening. Emotionally secure Nines are the most empathetic of the nine types, their gifts of support and friendship are given freely without expectation or stipulation. They withhold judgment and maintain a calm composure during tense situations, making them excellent mediators.

When stressed, Nines adopt characteristics from Six.

When relationships experience strain, Nines can disconnect and retreat inward, hoping that the problem will go away with time. Nines are also easily distracted, which can cause them to procrastinate on priority tasks. Curiously, they draw energy and creativity from the stress of looming deadlines. While Nines typically do not show anger, when stressed they can be passive-aggressive, withdrawn from others, and become quite stubborn.

How to relate: Since Nines can downplay their own needs with respect to the group's, be sure to provide space for them to share. Affirm them verbally; it charges their batteries. Their generosity can lead them to being overcommitted, so be careful with the quantity of your requests. If a Nine does say "no," thank them for their honesty.

Reflect: Which Enneagram type most aligns with you? Do those who know you best agree with your assessment? How can you embrace and utilize traits considered to be your strengths and weaknesses?

How Fusion Has Used the Enneagram

Our team has a healthy culture around knowing each other and exercising tangible and intangible skills for working in unison. We practice daily standups. We have weekly nonwork meetings during the day to chat over lunch or teach the rest of the team about a personal passion or hobby. We present personal learnings from conferences or workshops back to the group. In all of this, we are becoming more unified in our mindset while maximizing the diversity of our broad perspectives. The Enneagram is another tool toward this endeavor. By sharing our Enneagram type with the team and bringing others alongside our journey of self-discovery, we open up rich lines of communication and understanding that enrich our inter-team communication as well as our interaction with clients. A few examples of where our team has utilized the Enneagram:

- Structuring performance review conversations
- Establishing personal and work goals
- Providing feedback to team members, or hearing feedback from them
- Adapting to teammate working styles to enhance collaboration
- Understanding team member strengths and motivations behind behavior

You can take any number of free Enneagram tests online but know that they'll only be narrowing the options to types that likely align with you personally. From there, the work is on you to learn more about those types and see where you honestly believe you match. Don't be afraid of what may be perceived as "bad" traits. There is immense value and freedom in understanding your motivations and habits, especially the ones we can't seem to understand or change. Who you are is exactly who the world needs you to be so focus on becoming healthy and utilizing your gifts, strengths, and struggles toward impacting the world in your own unique way.

Enneagram Resources

- The Enneagram Institute
- Crystal <www.crystalknows.com/enneagram>
- *The Path Between Us: An Enneagram Journey to Healthy Relationships* by Suzanne Stabile[1]
- *The Complete Enneagram: 27 Paths to Greater Self-Knowledge* by Beatrice Chestnut[2]

Key Takeaways

Know Yourself First

Without an understanding of yourself, you receive and respond to others from a shifting foundation. By unlocking the source of your motivations and perspective, you can graciously respond to challenging individuals and joyfully collaborate with others' strengths. Start with a free Enneagram test to narrow the field of possible types. Then learn more about them to settle on which one feels like your core type.

Everyone Brings Value to the World

We all have those parts of ourselves that seem to cause trouble. When we understand what prompts others' reactions to us, we can harness the value in those personality traits and use them for greater impact. Likewise, viewing challenging attributes in others through a lens of context and understanding allows us to empathize and align toward common goals.

Give It Time

Perhaps you've steered clear of understanding your and others' internal motivations. It may take time to dig through the boundaries you've built up through life, and those boundaries may have altered the expression of your true self. Give it time. Be patient. Love yourself. In time you will begin to see the richness you—and others—hold inside. Consider this: There is a good side to parts of yourself that you—or others—have labeled as broken. The same applies to others in your life. What is the world missing out on by disregarding traits that have been augmented by stress?

CHAPTER 3

Inclusion and Diversity

By Sarah Konstantino

Exceptional leaders build and form teams that foster inclusive behaviors and represent the broad diversity surrounding us. Building an inclusive environment that allows teams to thrive is critical to harnessing the power of diversity within a team and business.

Introduction to Inclusion and Diversity

To capture the power of inclusion and diversity (I&D) within your team or organization, you must begin with understanding the nuances between the two and how bringing them together creates a multiplier effect that drives widespread impact.

Inclusion occurs when every single person in your team is valued, heard, respected, empowered, and feels a true sense of belonging. Inclusion goes beyond tolerating differences and a willingness to "accept" views that are different from yours. An inclusive team celebrates differences, seeks to understand them, and elevates each team member.

Diversity should be understood as uniquely different from inclusion (Figure 3.1); it encapsulates the full range of how an individual identifies.

Diversity has many facets including race, ethnicity, gender or gender identity, age, religious affiliation, and sexual orientation. It also includes people with differing educational backgrounds, personality types, cultural references, experiences, or physical abilities.

Inclusion and diversity allow us to utilize our full talents, ideas, and perspectives to ensure that our teams, organizations, and the world around us prosper. Individuals striving to bring their team to an elite level

INCLUSION   DIVERSITY

BELONGING   REPRESENTATION

FELT NOT SEEN

INDIVIDUALS ARE VALUED, RESPECTED & ACCEPTED

AUTHENTIC PARTICIPATION IN AN ORGANIZATION

EASILY MEASURED

WIDE ROSTER OF DIVERSE CHARACTERISTICS

REFLECTIVE OF POPULATIONS WE SERVE

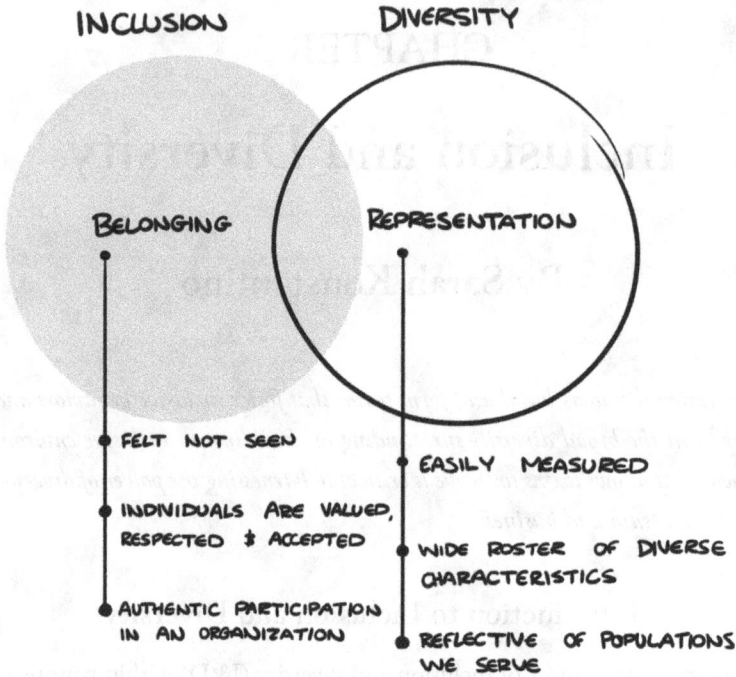

Figure 3.1 The intersection of inclusion and diversity

must integrate the core principles of I&D to effectively build and sustain a team representative of the wider world.

The Focus on Inclusion

According to SalesForce,

> Employees who say they're able to be their authentic self at work are nearly three times (2.8x) more likely to say they are proud to work for their company—and more than four times (4.4x) more likely to say they are empowered to perform their best work.[1]

While active investments in inclusion and diversity are critical to establishing a high-performing team, we encourage you to begin by examining practices at your organization that foster inclusion. If a strong, inclusive culture is not central to your team's ethos, it will be challenging to recruit, engage, and retain highly diverse talent.

Hiring

Inclusivity begins well before a candidate even joins your team. Imagine being a highly competent woman with years of experience, searching for your next role. You read through hundreds of job descriptions. Every time you get to the "requirements" section your heart drops, you don't have the right degree and aren't familiar with all five coding languages listed. You exit out of the description without applying and hope for a better fit with the next one. Data shows women are significantly less likely than men to apply for jobs they don't meet the qualifications for, meaning the way a job description is written may shrink your candidate pool.[2]

Writing an Inclusive Job Description

Research shows that 63 percent of jobseekers wouldn't apply for a job if they didn't understand the job title.[3] How you market your team, your company, and the work will be the first impression a candidate will have of you. In writing an inclusive job description, you will increase the chances of that potential candidate applying.

Three tips for creating an inclusive job description:

1. **Eliminate gendered language**

   There are explicit and implicit uses of gendered language that appear in job descriptions. The most explicit is the use of pronouns: "he should expect to work cross-functionally with multiple groups" or "she should actively engage with others throughout the process." Using specific pronouns in your job description may end up alienating individuals of the opposite sex and lead to an undiverse candidate pool. Instead, use "they/them," which also creates a more inclusive environment for individuals who do not adhere to the gender binary.

   Implicit language that may be gendered can show up in words like "rock star," "competitive," or "independent," which tend to attract and resonate more with male candidates, while words like "empathy," "collaboration," and "supportive," will tend to attract more female candidates Use more neutral language like "assist" to replace a feminized word like "support," or "inspired" to replace a more masculinized word like "driven."

2. Centralize a growth mindset

Many job descriptions focus on the importance of experience and a specific skill set. Instead of centralizing a list of must-have skills and experience, shift the emphasis to the importance of having a growth mindset. Outline your ideal candidate as one who is motivated to learn, take on challenges, and seek opportunities for growth.

3. Include your team's commitment to I&D

Explicitly demonstrate to prospective candidates your team's commitment to I&D by including a statement that highlights how you build inclusive practices in the workplace. Emphasize that you welcome diverse candidates' perspectives and experiences and encourage them to support the evolution of your team.

If you do not have a statement that explicitly highlights these commitments, work with your broader team to ideate how your commitment to I&D shows up in your day-to-day work.

Facilitating an Inclusive Interview

Interviews can be challenging. They are often led by two to three people who have been chosen to represent the interests of a much larger team, and they tend to be highly focused on culture fit.

The historical pillars of the interview tend to lead to a noninclusive experience for both the interviewees as well as the broader team that the interviewers are selected to represent. These practices hinder candidates' ability to showcase their skills and experience, while also limiting their understanding of their potential experience on the team.

> **Reflect:** What is your current interview experience like for a candidate? Do you enable them to gain a full understanding of their potential future work experience? How might you structure your interview to ensure it is reflective of the actual work experience?

Creating a highly inclusive interview process allows both candidates and teammates to feel part of the process.

Full Team Representation

In our team, we strive to include everyone in the interview process. We understand that relationships drive performance and want to ensure each member of the team has a say as we expand. Our interview process has four phases, and each team member is involved in at least one phase. These include collaborative working sessions, a candidate presentation, a behavioral interview, and a one-on-one. We have one teammate who is responsible for ensuring each member of the team is involved in at least one phase of the interview process. He sends out calendar holds for each of the 30-minute interview timeslots, and our team runs like a smoothly operating machine, flowing in and out of the interview room to engage with a potentially new teammate.

You can begin creating a highly inclusive interview by establishing a structure that allows a candidate to interact with as many members of the team as possible. While this may sound potentially overwhelming for a candidate, there are ways to do it that enhances the candidate's understanding of the team and its diversity. Leveraging a full-team approach also allows everyone to provide their unique perspective on the candidate during the full-team candidate debrief process, which we will cover later in the chapter.

Preventing Bias

Historically, a best practice for an interview is to share an individual candidate's resume with the interview panel. However, this could potentially lead to a biased view of the candidate based on several factors: their name, background, GPA, previous experience, degree, and so on. To mitigate conscious and unconscious bias, avoid sharing the candidate's resume with the interviewers. Allow them to get a full picture of the individual and their skillset through the multipart interview process.

Multipart Interview Approach

To structure your inclusive interview, break down the core components of the role.

> **Reflect:** What are some responsibilities this individual will have? What are the tools or ways of working you expect this individual to learn or leverage to be successful?

After outlining the above, reflect on how you might convert these elements into an interview segment.

Example: A core responsibility of this role is working closely with clients to understand their needs and translate those needs into requirements for a collaborative workshop.

Interview Approach: Roleplay a client intake and provide your candidate background on the client and their problem area. Have them conduct the intake and guide the conversation with a goal of understanding the client's requirements.

There are many benefits to establishing a multipart and varied interview process rooted in the core role and responsibilities of the job you are hiring for. First, it allows your candidate to experience how your team works and collaborates on a day-to-day basis. Second, it focuses on identifying a growth mindset. If your interview team teaches the candidate something new during one of the interview segments, you will be able to assess their joy for learning and how they process and apply new material. Third, this approach enables the candidate to interact with multiple members of your team, showcasing its full range of diversity. Finally, it allows your full team to assess an individual from multiple lenses. There may be aspects of the interview where the candidate shines and could be a learning moment for your team. On the other hand, the candidate could be unsuccessful at aspects of the interview, but demonstrate a growth mindset. The multipart approach allows your team to see an interviewee from multiple lenses and to make a highly informed decision together.

The process I went through on the Fusion team was the most intensive, and the most inclusive I have ever had. My interview was three hours long during this time I met and collaborated with every member of the team. I appreciated having the opportunity to demonstrate my talent and experience across areas that were important to the team. I also experienced their day-to-day operations of the team as well as how the culture it embodied.

Inclusive Candidate Review: Collective Decision-Making

Over many years, our team has crafted and evolved a Team DNA structure, which defines what skills, characteristics and experiences make up a holistically strong team. Our DNA is made of multiple categories including Design, Strategy, Systems Thinking, and Leadership Presence. As we work collaboratively together, our expectation is not for each teammate to be fully competent in every area. Instead, we use the DNA to define where we as a team have room to grow.

The final stage in the inclusive interview process is the candidate review, scoring, and making a joint decision, as a team, if an offer should be extended. To facilitate a fair and inclusive review process, it is critical to have a set scoring system for which the collective team will rank the candidate(s) against.

In developing the scoring system, we recommend first cataloging your core team values or team DNA—what values does your team have that are critical to success?

Next leverage that values catalog and align it to your core interview segments. Document how each segment tests for or represents a subset of those core values.

Once you have understood and documented those core values and aligned them to the segments of your interview process, your team can leverage a scoring system (1 to 5 or 1 to 10) to assess the candidate. Keep in mind not all individuals on the team would have attended every part of the interview process, so individuals are asked to score on a given subset of the values based on their experience with the candidate.

After the initial scoring is complete, the team goes through one interview segment at a time and hears from the respective teammates in that portion of the interview. They reflect on the candidate's performance within their segment as it relates to the core values of the team. We find that the debriefing process allows the whole team to get a full perspective of the end-to-end interview. It allows individuals on the team to raise questions they may have about the candidate and have those answered by another member, who may have seen a core skill demonstrated during a different segment. The informed discussion allows for a final scoring in which the team ranks a candidate to determine the next steps.

The next step, whether your team is extending an offer or not, is critical to delivering an inclusive end-to-end hiring process. Within the final scoring process, our team assesses a candidate on the following scale of 1–4:

4: Hire the candidate immediately for our team.

3: Strong Candidate: Discuss next steps or follow up on open questions.

2: Strong Candidate for a different team in our company: Make an introduction.

1: Strong candidate for a company within our network: Identify companies and make an introduction.

We know that a highly inclusive interview asks a potential candidate to invest a lot, as it includes a multipart interview incorporating many different members of a given team. To carry your inclusive principles forward, it is important to recognize and appreciate the time an individual has dedicated to the interview.

The final scoring process delivers value back to a candidate in the form of a job offer or an introduction somewhere in our collective network that aligns better with their strengths and talent. Additionally, a highly inclusive interview process also provides feedback to the candidate on the strengths that were identified as well as areas for improvement. This feedback should never be about culture-fit, but rather specific areas as they relate to the role.

Training and Onboarding

The training and onboarding experience for a new individual is critical to their success in the role and their retention within your team. Research shows that "69 percent of employees are more likely to stay with a company for three years if they experienced great onboarding."[4] Adopting a highly inclusive interview process is step one to ensuring your new employees feel valued as they join your organization. Your next step is to establish a highly inclusive and engaging training and onboarding. According to *Onboarding New Employees* author, Dr. Talya Bauer,

Research and conventional wisdom both suggest that employees get about 90 days to prove themselves in a new job. The faster new hires feel welcome and prepared for their jobs, the faster they will be able to successfully contribute to the firm's mission.[5]

Examine your process through the lens of inclusivity to help ensure your newly hired teammate feels connected, prepared, and empowered in their role.

Connection

Connection is a critical part of welcoming a new hire into your collective team. Known for her research on shame, vulnerability, and leadership, Dr. Brené Brown defines connection as "the energy that exists between people when they feel seen, heard, and valued; when they can give and receive without judgment; and when they derive sustenance and strength from the relationship."[6] An onboarding mentor is a great way to make your new employees feel connected from Day 1 and continue to guide them through their first three months. On our team, the onboarding mentor supports the new hire in getting their computer set up on Day 1, walks the new hire through their 30-60-90-day plan, and are available for one-on-one support and training throughout the onboarding experience.

The mentor you assign to support a new hire's onboarding should be someone who has deep knowledge of the team and company's processes and values and can readily share those insights. They should also be an individual who can actively listen, with an interest in really getting to know the goals and aspirations of the new hire, helping them align those passions to opportunities within the team. Finally, the mentor should be someone who can answer with honesty and help the new employee work through any challenges. They can assist in finding the right tools, information, and context to support their first three months as they ramp up on the team and within the organization. The mentor's goal is to establish an authentic connection with the new hire and lay the foundation for a positive and inclusive onboarding experience.

Creating connections with other team members will contribute to an inclusive environment. Encourage the new teammate to set up one-on-ones within the first two weeks. To make these one-on-ones effective, provide your new hire with specific questions to ask related to your team's processes, values, or tools. The structured one-on-ones will fast-track the new employee's understanding of the team, prepare them for their role, help facilitate connection, and reduce the pressure on the onboarding mentor during the preparation phase.

Preparation

There are two major areas that a team and mentor should focus on during the first 90 days to ensure a new team member feels adequately prepared and set up for success.

First, prepare the newest team member to be an active contributor in their role from their first week. You should encourage them to engage with the subject matter and the skills they are expected to develop on the team. The most effective way to do this is to actively involve them in new or ongoing projects with more seasoned team members. Make sure this experience is as inclusive as possible by encouraging them to ask questions about the process, while also taking the time to explain the "why" behind decisions that are made to advance the project.

Second, involve the new team member as an active contributor to ongoing team dynamics, culture, and rituals (more on rituals in Chapter 7, "Intentional Communication"). Actively help them learn the rituals within the team culture. Provide them a safe place to receive an overview of what the rituals are, explain why the team has put them in place, and how they contribute to strong team performance. You can also provide examples of how the ritual comes to life within the team and when your new teammate should expect to experience it. Ensure that they feel welcome to ask questions about why certain rituals exist and invite them to support the evolution of team dynamics.

After learning the rituals and understanding the culture, ask if they see an opportunity for improvement. This invitation to co-create and evolve team rituals supports a highly inclusive culture and helps take your team's collaboration to the next level.

Inclusive Leadership

"The behaviors a leader demonstrates make up to a 70 percent difference as to whether an individual within their team will report feeling included."[7]

Transform Yourself

The foundational element to establishing and maximizing an inclusive culture within your team or organization is a demonstrated commitment and follow-through from leadership.

Inclusive and thoughtful leadership is imperative to driving organizational growth and performance. An inclusive leader sets the tone and enables diverse individuals within an organization to feel included and authentically themselves. When individuals feel included, they speak up more, take initiative, and collaborate more effectively. This leads to increased employee engagement and retention and delivers outsized business performance. Top performers in today's work environment expect organizations to have thoughtful approaches to I&D, and also look for how teams build inclusive practices into their day-to-day responsibilities.

To become an inclusive leader, you can take steps to adopt new values that allow you to become more grounded, intentional, and humble.

Be Grounded. Being grounded means you are present and connected with yourself and those around you. You are balanced and stay centered even in the most trying moments. Being grounded allows you to focus on what you stand for.

> **Reflect:** What do you stand for?

Be Intentional. Being intentional means you take actions and make decisions based on what is most important to you. To be intentionally inclusive means you seek to thoughtfully engage everyone's full potential.

> **Reflect:** How do you understand personal motivations in others and activate them toward action?

Be Humble.   Being humble means you are open to growth and learning from others. You prioritize relationships over your need to be right and you learn by listening to others.

> **Reflect:** Do you want to build relationships, or do you want to be right?

You need to grow yourself before you can support others in their growth. Driving systemic changes within an organization starts with creating change in yourself.

Transform Your Organization

Inclusive teams begin with inclusive leaders. Becoming an inclusive leader requires some foundational behavior changes that may feel at odds with the status quo in a more traditional organization. These changes ask you to be courageous and willing to take an iterative approach to find the right structures to amplify inclusion within your team.

Within our organization, we have created monthly leadership equity, inclusion, and diversity engagement sessions. These sessions provide a safe space for leaders to explore what it means to be a more inclusive and how to effectively engage their teams in topics that have not historically been addressed in the workplace.

To begin a cultural transformation, review your team's processes and approaches through the lens of four key behaviors for transformational, inclusive leadership[8]:

Inclusive Leaders Break Down Barriers

Take conscious steps to review current practices and identify and rectify the barriers in place that exclude individuals.

> **Reflect:** Think about your leadership succession pipeline, do you have diverse representation across your future leaders?

Inclusive Leaders Welcome Individual Contribution

Embody an approach that is open to diverse perspectives, seeking active feedback from teammates you typically do not receive feedback from.

> **Reflect:** How might you create a process in which you can gather rapid feedback from multiple parties?

Inclusive Leaders Take an Eco-Systemic Approach

Seek out opportunities to experience the system from the perspectives of others to gain insight into the impact of an upcoming decision.

> **Reflect:** What processes are in place to understand the impact on the frontline when changes are made in the organization?

Inclusive Leaders Promote Full Engagement in Decision-Making

Invite diverse thinkers into the decision-making process and allow them to shape your team or organization's future.

> **Reflect:** When was the last time you invited someone new into your "circle of trust" when big decisions were made?

Review your current processes and identify which behaviors create the greatest impact. If you are struggling to pinpoint the opportunities, invite others to give you feedback on the current processes and their experiences within the organization. Implementing these four behaviors will not happen overnight; success will take thoughtful planning and require change management.

Exceptional leaders build teams that foster inclusive behaviors and represent the broad diversity surrounding us. Building an inclusive environment that allows diverse teams to thrive is critical to harnessing the power of diversity within a team and business.

Key Takeaways

Culture Shifts Toward Inclusion Must Be Supported by Leaders

Investments in inclusion and diversity are maximized when championed by core leaders within the organization; it requires sustained support from leaders to create lasting change. Hold a workshop with your team: Identify what inclusion means to them and ideate steps the team could take to become even more inclusive.

Inclusive Hiring Practices Improve Team Diversity

Reflect on your team's recruitment and hiring practices, examine the processes, and identify opportunities to improve inclusion. Leverage your team to identify 3–5 new avenues to recruit new talent and begin reaching out to form new relationships.

Inclusive Onboarding Increases Retention

The first three months are critical. Ensure that your new hires have a highly inclusive experience within your team or organization. Match your new hire with an onboarding mentor and gather feedback throughout the process from both to identify successes and opportunities for improvement.

CHAPTER 4

Virtuous Cycles

Creating Positive Patterns of Success

By Ryan Tyler

Chapter 1, "The Formula is Simple: Purpose, Passion, and People," mentioned that we are an integral part of a bigger system, fighting to make an impact on the world. This led the author, Colby Champagne, to describe the importance of virtuous cycles and how a chain of events can lead to successive desirable outcomes. Colby mentioned that the positive impact virtuous cycles can have on the employee experience, and this chapter expands on the importance of virtuous cycles and their effect on your team.

Creating Positive Patterns of Success

Virtuous cycles are rooted in the process of systems thinking (Figure 4.1). Human Resource Consulting Agency, TalentTelligent, LLC, defines systems thinking as a set of processes and steps with built-in feedback loops.[1] These feedback loops keep the process going until the desired outcome is achieved. By continuing to progress through the series of loops, the team continues to learn, creating momentum and increasing expertise each time they progress through the cycle.

A virtuous cycle can be small, operate over days, or drive a company's strategy for decades. Within teams, virtuous cycles can happen through new learnings or repeating a series of tasks to advance a common goal. We are used to seeing them in our team's underlying processes. If you are part of a technology team that implements Agile methodologies, you

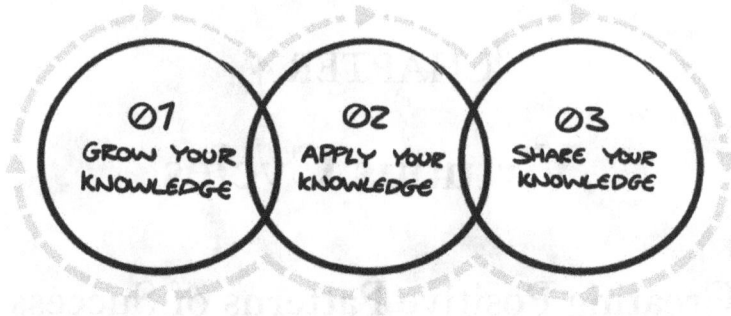

Figure 4.1 **A virtuous cycle**

may have observed the momentum gained from a successful sprint or a program increment (PI) carrying the team forward and bringing additional momentum into the next iteration of a product. If you are part of a strategy team that incorporates Business Process Management (BPM) best practices into day-to-day operations, you may have noticed stronger outcomes and measurable results as the team progressed from one year to the next. Across approaches, an event with a positive outcome can lead to another. This creates greater opportunities for exploration and achieving success by mastering processes, discipline, and so on, resulting in the ability to teach others and pass down what has been learned based on observation and experience.

This chapter explores how to apply the principles of virtuous cycles, systems thinking, and growth mindsets within your team to achieve outcomes leading to greater success. I will provide insight from my own experience based on teams that I have been a part of, give examples of models and frameworks that can be applied to accelerate the process, and reference different authors, influencers, and books that have inspired me to create my own positive patterns of success.

Grow Your Knowledge

I was not a great student and struggled with understanding the value of learning new things. I was more interested in pursuing my own interests and becoming an artist. Over time, I embraced my passions and learned to appreciate new techniques within my artistic practice that created new possibilities. These were the first steps in creating positive patterns of success.

Aspire for More and Change Behavior

In her book, *Mindset: The New Psychology of Success*,[2] Carol Dweck articulates the difference between a fixed mindset and a growth mindset.[3] She explains that individuals with a fixed mindset believe that they will never learn more than what they know, keeping them from reaching their full potential. Dweck writes that individuals with a growth mindset (Figure 4.2) push the boundaries of what they currently know and challenge themselves to identify new opportunities. Similarly, leadership author and researcher, Brené Brown, tells us that "Vulnerability is not knowing victory or defeat; it's understanding the necessity of both; it's engaging. It's being all in."[4] "Engaging" and "being all in" are keys to a growth mindset.

Leverage a Growth Mindset to Overcome Challenges

The same principles apply to your team's approach to challenges. Several distinct moments allowed me to mature and appreciate the value of learning. Instances where I felt embarrassed or defeated became opportunities because it became easier to make a change than continue in that negative state. One example occurred when I was part of an engagement team—I spent hours alongside my colleagues responding with care to an in-depth request for proposal (RFP). We learned that we had not made the final list. A second instance happened during a two-year engagement. Halfway through, our team was asked to step aside for another, more qualified team to complete the remaining work. When moments like these happen, take the opportunity to learn from the experience. These

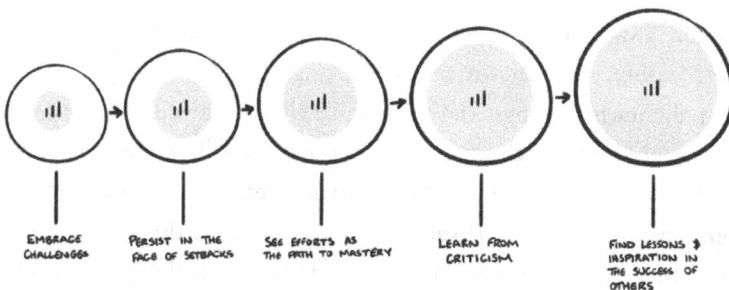

EMBRACE CHALLENGES   PERSIST IN THE FACE OF SETBACKS   SEE EFFORTS AS THE PATH TO MASTERY   LEARN FROM CRITICISM   FIND LESSONS & INSPIRATION IN THE SUCCESS OF OTHERS

Figure 4.2 Growth mindset model

lessons will make the team better prepared for whatever comes next. In the words of Jocko Willink and Leif Babin, the authors of *Extreme Ownership: How U.S. Navy SEALS Lead and Win*,[5] "GOOD. More time to get better."[6]

Be Curious and Explore; Be Aware of Possibilities; and Expand Your Horizons

In his book, *Principles*, Ray Dalio writes about how to make money in the market. His process is a virtuous cycle: Start by setting audacious goals, fail, learn the principles, improve, and set more audacious goals. As the chapters begin to unfold, Ray outlines how these same processes and principles can be applied in all aspects of life. One important principle is "Make Being Open-minded a Habit."[7]

Being curious, keeping an open mind, and learning new things allow for rapid growth and improve our understanding of what might be possible if we are willing to expand our horizons and try something new. In early 2011, I was part of a team that was introduced to Apple's iOS Human-Interface Guidelines for mobile devices. Over the course of several months, we researched the possibilities of mobile design and how to create exceptional applications for the iPhone and the newly released iPad. This effort helped us become one of the top mobile design resources in the company, providing new opportunities to deliver meaningful experiences to our clients and the customers they served. We worked as a team to move past what we knew of traditional mediums of design and explored other possibilities. Our efforts opened once closed doors, allowing us to bring new offerings to market.

There are models and frameworks to accelerate this process of learning and growth within your own team. Objectives, Goals, Strategies, and Measures, also known as OGSM (Figure 4.3), are helpful in creating alignment amongst the team and help individuals become aware of what needs to be achieved and how the team will progress.[8] Creating an OGSM for your team involves everyone defining the vision. Aspirational and tactical plans help accomplish the objective through milestone goal-setting and the creation of strategies to get there, along with metrics to track and measure the success of the team's efforts.

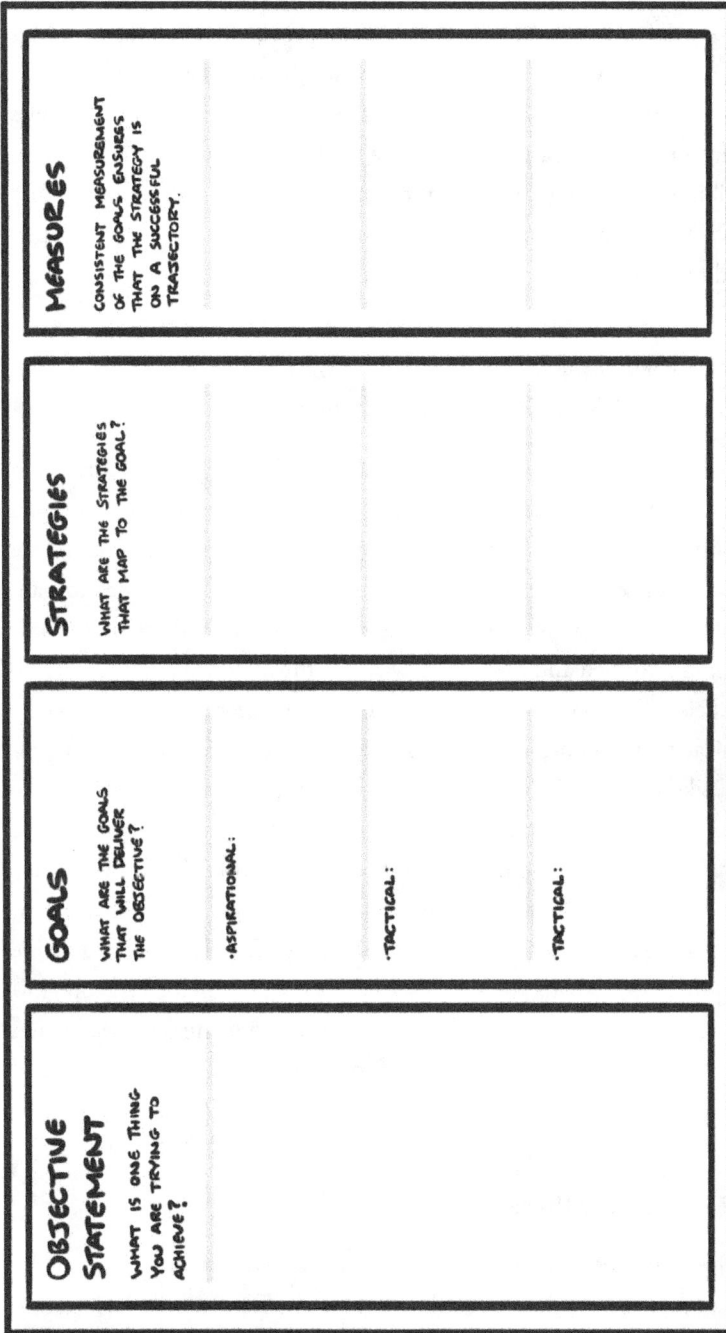

OBJECTIVE STATEMENT

WHAT IS ONE THING YOU ARE TRYING TO ACHIEVE?

GOALS

WHAT ARE THE GOALS THAT WILL DELIVER THE OBJECTIVE?

- ASPIRATIONAL:

- TACTICAL:

- TACTICAL:

STRATEGIES

WHAT ARE THE STRATEGIES THAT MAP TO THE GOAL?

MEASURES

CONSISTENT MEASUREMENT OF THE GOALS ENSURES THAT THE STRATEGY IS ON A SUCCESSFUL TRAJECTORY.

Figure 4.3 OGSM framework

OGSM Framework

Utilizing a framework like OGSM or other proven methodologies creates alignment, allowing team members to suggest new strategies and metrics for how they will accomplish their objectives. Like other examples of virtuous cycles, teams can progress by having an open mind to new possibilities, learning from insights, measuring their opportunities and successes, and challenging themselves to start the cycle again with an open mind to the future.

Make a Commitment to Learning by Doing Research, Speaking to Others, and Finding Mentors

User experience (UX) and user interface (UI) designers conduct research to understand the current state, the perceived challenges, and the proposed resolution of a given situation. As a leader of UX and product experience (PX) design teams, we use a variety of research methodologies to gain insights, build empathy, and apply the data to recommend a path forward, bringing informed and measurable value to the intended audience.

Nielsen Norman Group, a world leader in research-based UX, communicates the importance that research plays in the overall design process. Like the process outlined by Ray Dalio in the book *Principles*, the Nielsen Norman Group follows a design thinking methodology to enable their clients to create differentiated experiences within the market.[9] They begin by defining the problem and progress through phases of research, ideation, creation, implementation, and testing. They loop back to define new problems, starting the process again. "Design thinking" (Figure 4.4) is another notable example of a virtuous cycle and identifies research as a key phase that helps the team identify opportunities to create better and more engaging experiences.

Design Thinking Process

Incorporating design thinking in my day-to-day role and within the teams I manage provides valuable insight and offers a model for creating repeatable patterns of success. When my team mentors individuals at the early stages of their career, we ask them to learn about the various roles

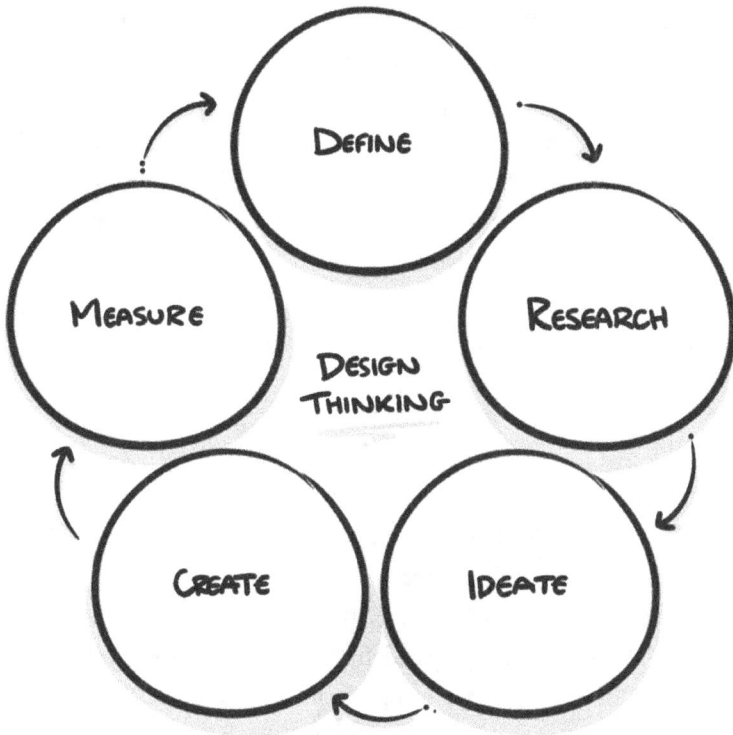

Figure 4.4 Design thinking process

that exist within their field. This exploration exposes them to different possibilities and creates a change in behavior to aspire for more.

Like individuals, teams can benefit from speaking with others who have domain knowledge in a specific field and seeking mentors to help them grow. The team might want to reach a new level of maturity in their discipline or role within the company. Or, they might need mentorship to strengthen communication, learn a shared skill, or navigate rough waters. Identifying a mentor for your team can be a helpful way to accelerate growth, create goals, and build shared experiences.

Take time to think about the mentors you have had in the past, who supported you as an individual or within a team. Depending on their style of coaching, they might help you *identify* areas of opportunity you wish to focus on, *research* topics related to any blockers that might impede progress, *ideate* solutions based on new or existing insights, *create* plans to advance, *measure* success and, *impact* over time.

Within virtuous cycles, growing knowledge is the first step in the process and must be completed before proceeding to the second step, applying knowledge. Learning can be its own virtuous cycle, but we must have the discipline to proceed to the next step, "applying knowledge," to achieve success and sustain growth.

> **Reflect:** Why do you want to experience new levels of learning and growth?

Apply Your Knowledge

Athletes continuously develop the skills to perform as professionals in their sport. Their commitment to develop and increase their skills began in their youth, and at each stage of their career, they get progressively better by being mentally prepared for the next opportunity, repeating skill-based challenges, and creating small wins to gain confidence as they progress through their journey as professional athletes. The same approach can be applied to your team's approach to new challenges.

In the previous section, I mentioned the importance of changing behavior as part of learning. Now, we will explore how it applies to building skills and how small, incremental changes over time help those changes become new habits for you and your team.

Achievement Mindset: Skill Building and Drive

BJ Fogg, the author of *Tiny Habits: The small changes that change everything*,[10] says that successfully changing a behavior requires starting small. This section explores this concept and shares examples applicable to teams.

Several years ago, I was part of a team that developed a new web application focused on health and wellness programs. Part of the underlying experience was a model for changing behavior that supported individuals as they took ownership of their health decisions. The program focused on three phases of progression: starting with awareness, continuing through levels of skill building, and concluding with proficiency. My team and I learned that the same patterns of success in this program could apply to different situations, so we incorporated these learnings into our own approach to building personal and team success.

For example, new consultants often join our team as a cohort. Over several weeks and months, veteran team members teach the cohort a core set of frameworks, best practices, and methodologies to help accelerate our clients as they progress toward achieving their goal. Each new lesson provides the cohort with an in-depth review of the framework, past examples of how and when it should be applied, and a common talk track to ensure consistency in how frameworks are introduced and delivered in practice. Before new consultants can lead a client or session participants through a framework, they must first demonstrate their knowledge by presenting the materials to their peers and leaders. New consultants prepare their sessions and incorporate feedback, then undergo the process again, building their skills and putting their knowledge into practice.

Go Deep and Geek Out: Apply Learnings to Other Problems and Opportunities

Frameworks are excellent tools that drive new thinking and accelerate focused action. Our team makes use of over 150 different frameworks to help our clients solve problems. These frameworks are rooted in different methodologies, including Lean, Agile, Human-Centered Design (HCD), Business Model Generation, Value Proposition-Design, and many others. We create and leverage frameworks to help individuals and teams prioritize, articulate, and apply their thinking.

As I familiarized myself with the frameworks and their underlying operating model, I explored how these frameworks could help solve other problems beyond the original scope of work. For example, Objectives and Key Results (OKRs) is a popular business framework for communicating goals in organizations that want to connect the company, teams, and personal objectives to measurable results. OKRs enable businesses to create alignment, understand the strategy, and track measurable results across

OBJECTIVE & KEY RESULTS
EXAMPLE

USER STORY:

AS A CONSUMER, I WANT TO
BE ABLE TO SEE A LIST OF
FILTERED & SORTED PRODUCTS,
SO THAT I CAN MAKE MY
SELECTION EASIER & FASTER.

OBJECTIVES:

REDUCE TIME IN THE DECISION
MAKING PROCESS.

KEY RESULTS:

1. REDUCE THE OVERALL TIME
ON TASK BY 25%.
2. INCREASE CONSUMER SATISFACTION
& THE NET PROMOTOR SCORE (NPS)
BY 10.
3. INCREASE SALES BY 5% BY
GETTING THE CONSUMER
THROUGH THE END-TO-END
SALES FUNNEL.

Figure 4.5 UX design and the OKR framework

a product or service. Our team has applied OKRs to help advance the creation of UX designs (Figure 4.5).

Design can be subjective, and others' opinions are important. This can be hard for new designers and design teams to accept. OKRs and Key Performance Indicators (KPIs) can be applied to support the team's design decisions and convey to their business partners the measurable value of the recommended experience. While OKRs and KPIs were not developed to support the creation of graphical interfaces and experience design, by "geeking out" on the framework and exploring how it might apply in other situations, our team created experiences that are measurable and rooted in communicating the value of the design.

This is just one example of how our team applied frameworks to other use cases. It is crucial to make time for geeking out, as doing so will evolve your team from a fixed opinion or mindset to a growth mindset.

Take Time to Build Proficiency and Outperform Yourself

Jiro Dreams of Sushi[11] is a documentary that examines the discipline of three-Michelin-star chef, Jiro Ono, who has dedicated his entire life to achieving perfection in simple yet eloquent dishes.

> *I do the same thing over and over, improving bit by bit. There is always a yearning to achieve more. I'll continue to climb, trying to reach the top, but no one knows where the top is.*
>
> —Jiro Ono[12]

At age 94, he has accumulated a lifetime of skill and experience, resulting in his status as one of the greatest sushi chefs in modern times.

I am not yet an expert in my craft like Jiro Ono, but I can relate to his guidance about immersing yourself in your work and falling in love with what you do. Even if we love what we do, we will face challenges as we pursue mastery. A growth mindset provides a framework to persist in the face of such setbacks. Embracing a growth mindset in reflecting on past challenges has helped me understand them as catalysts for growth in my career.

Each year, our team sets elevated expectations for what we hope to achieve. This ensures that we continue to grow and challenge ourselves, avoiding complacency. It also allows us to expand our potential impact on others. We have a unique responsibility as a team working for a health-care company that supports millions and helps them live healthier lives. Therefore, we consider what we can achieve, and for whom if we attain a certain level of proficiency. As Jiro Ono says, "No one knows where the top is." The only way we can find out is by outperforming our own expectations of what can be achieved.

Within virtuous cycles, applying knowledge is the second step in the process and must be completed before we can proceed to the third step: sharing our knowledge. In this section, I talked about how applying what we have learned can further grow and lead to additional levels of success; but we must be willing to expand to new problem areas to achieve a new level of proficiency. This carries a similar risk to the "gaining knowledge" phase; we can get stuck in this part of the cycle. Even Jiro Ono knew that he had to make time to pass down his knowledge to his son and other apprentices to continue to try and reach the pinnacle of perfection.

> **Reflect**: How can you find new ways to put your own learnings into practice?

Share Your Knowledge

If you want to build a ship, don't drum up people to collect wood and don't assign them tasks and work but, rather, teach them to long for the endless immensity of the sea.[13]

—Antoine de Saint-Exupery

Throughout this chapter, I have cited several inspiring authors whose level of insight and domain knowledge has helped me grow personally and professionally. Their ability to excel in their field and share their knowledge is crucial to the final phase of growth in virtuous cycles.

Develop Others: Lead Change and Transitions

Part of our organization's core values is the concept of the leadership shadow. It entails being mindful of the shadow that you cast on those around you. How do they perceive you when you are leading? Do they see you as someone who puts others first and leads with integrity?

These questions have always been at the forefront of my mind, especially when I make decisions about my career and when leading my team. As I have matured as a teacher, manager, and leader within our company, I have come to understand that the shadow I cast today will influence the shadow they cast in the future. As Peter Senge mentions in his book, *The Fifth Discipline, The Art of Practice of the Learning Organization,* "The next generation of leaders . . . have the distinctive ability to see the flaws in current models . . . and the courage to create something new. When young people develop basic leadership and collaborative learning skills, they can be a formidable force for change."[14] These future leaders need guidance and opportunities to lead.

Over the last four years, our team has led an early career program. We worked with hundreds of individuals, teaching them our frameworks, coaching them on professional development skills, helping them build their personal brand, and preparing them for whatever their "next" may be. It has been one of our team goals, referring to our own OGSM, to inspire these individuals to achieve their own success.

To inspire others, you must first become an example of positive change and establish a level of expectation for others to follow. Four years ago, our team did not have all the answers for how to inspire others. We went through our own virtuous cycle to shift from each person's vision of the team to a shared vision. We continuously learned from others, applied that knowledge in different situations, and led a team of support resources toward a shared vision, ultimately achieving our desired results. We focused on the best way to teach, guide, assist, connect, and protect the growth of our early career team members and prioritized outcomes over output. This created a model of leadership that sets precedence in the way we operate and how our team members might lead in the future.

Taking this approach can have a considerable influence on "Why" and "How" we share our knowledge with others. We developed a genuine appreciation for sharing our learnings and experiences, which fuels our progression through the various parts of the virtuous cycle.

Pass Down the Learning and How You Applied It; Individuals; Teams

In her book, *Extreme You; Stand Up. Stand Out. Kick Ass*, Sarah Robb O'Hagan argues that when you become a leader and want to bring out the excellence in others, your most vital role is as a mentor and supporter.[15] Aside from giving back to others, mentoring can improve communication and intrapersonal skills, help develop leadership qualities, increase confidence, and extend our organizational network.

I have had four mentors in my professional career, and each played a significant role in my development. They spent time asking questions, providing insights, making recommendations, and instructing me in new ways of thinking. Whether it was deciding if I should pursue a new career path, talking about the challenges of finding a work-life balance, or providing me with a level of radical candor when I needed to hear something to grow, they invested time and resources in me.

As internal consultants within our company, our team can meet new people all the time, especially individuals who are new in their career. This provides us with a unique opportunity in which we are often asked for guidance on a variety of topics. We are often asked how we got to where we are today and what guidance could help accelerate them. Whether you are guiding individuals or teams, the following recommendations are best practices that we have used:

The first step is to make time and practice *being here now*. Simply said, when you invest time in being a mentor, be present and pay attention to what is being said. Listen to the problems and challenges they are seeking support for and have empathy for them. A mentor is first a listener and then a communicator. Once you understand how you can best support them, walk them through the steps of a virtuous cycle. Share your experiences, connect them to your circle of contacts, and recommend books, training modules, conferences to attend, or resources where they can learn from others. After they have gained knowledge, think about how you can be an advocate and help them find opportunities to put their learnings into practice. Speak with other leaders and teams on their behalf, and challenge your mentee to apply their learnings in their day-to-day work or even take on additional work outside their role. We believe that it is good to challenge your mentees, as it will help in their growth. If you follow this guidance, make sure that you challenge them in a safe space where it is okay to fall a little short as they build their confidence. In the final stage of the virtuous cycle, encourage them to apply what they have learned and teach others, perhaps as a guest speaker, as a coach, or as a mentor themselves.

Becoming a mentor is a fantastic way to give back and pay it forward, just as others have done for you.

Reflect: What can you do to help others as you complete your own virtuous cycle of learning?

Get Ready for Your Next

We started the chapter by defining virtuous cycles and discussing the value of a systems thinking approach and the benefits of having a growth mindset. We explored three distinct stages of virtuous cycles, starting with growing your knowledge by aspiring for more and changing your behaviors, being curious, taking on new challenges, and making a commitment to learning. We moved into the second stage, applying your knowledge, building your skills through an achievement mindset, going deep and geeking out, and taking time to build proficiency and outperform yourself. We ended with the last stage of virtuous cycles: developing others, leading change, and, finally, passing down your learnings by becoming a mentor.

I encourage you to continue to challenge yourself and your team to implement some of the processes and frameworks listed within the chapter. Remember, with each virtuous cycle, there is always a beginning and an end, and the end is always the beginning of something new!

Key Takeaways

Grow Your Knowledge

Change your behavior by challenging yourself to learn something new.

Apply Your Knowledge

As with professional athletes, you can only get better and grow your skills through continuous practice and repetition.

Share Your Knowledge

Once you have mastered your discipline, consider becoming a mentor to others, sharing what you have learned to accelerate their journey.

CHAPTER 5

Stay Curious

By Sarah Witty

Individuals that stay curious bring an edge to their team, and teams that give individuals space to pursue that curiosity create positive work environments and better outcomes. Valuing hyper-learning practices increases the efficiency and impact of fulfilling our curiosity for ourselves and for our teams.

Why Is Satisfying Curiosity Important?

An inquisitive nature and a drive to learn new things and new ways of doing things are essential for making improvements to the current state and for adapting to shifts in our personal and working lives. It leads us to ponder powerful questions such as "What if" and is grounded in a propensity to always question "Why." Most of us were at some point in our lives very curious beings. The "5 Whys" problem-solving framework, a concept frequently used in meeting rooms to conduct root cause analysis, is intuitive to any 4-year-old interrogating their parent. As we get older and leave formal learning institutions, many of us lack the space and encouragement to be curious. Like any muscle, curiosity deteriorates without use, and we need to create intentional programs to train it.

Curiosity falls short when it ends at the open questions. Without clear guidance and support on what to do when curiosity is piqued, we can find ourselves in a tailspin and wasting time without finding a satisfying conclusion. Questions can go unanswered because we don't know where to start, we get lost in a web of information without a clear path to follow, or we fear that knowing the answer is more troublesome than ignorance. This limits our own growth and our team's potential improvement.

An effective team can recognize the pitfalls of wandering curiosity and replace them with the benefits of productive curiosity. People with productive curiosity question how processes work and figure out how they could be improved; they are proactive in finding answers when others don't even know to ask the question yet. Several techniques in this chapter will improve our capacity to learn that help teams develop the skills necessary to cultivate a culture of productive curiosity.

How Do You Turn Wandering Curiosity into Productive Curiosity?

Hyper-learning is the critical skill that will propel you and your team toward productive curiosity. It is the human capacity to learn, unlearn, and relearn continually to adapt to the speed of change.[1] Hyper-learning is not only the ability to quickly learn in the moment but also the ability to apply that new knowledge. It is about going above and beyond through the internalization of knowledge and the ability to synthesize multiple data sources in meaningful and new ways. It makes curiosity actionable. It makes curiosity productive. It makes curiosity valuable.

There is an unprecedented and ever-growing mass of content available to us and our expertise cannot afford to be static. As Edward O. Wilson notes in his book, *Hyper-Learning*, "We are drowning in information while starving for wisdom. The world henceforth will be run by synthesizers, people able to put together the right information at the right time, think critically, and make important choices wisely." Even with this awareness, it can be difficult to know where to invest our time and effort to ensure we are able to deliver value. Which curiosities do we pursue? As the Greek philosopher Heraclitus posits that change is the only constant in life. Equipping ourselves with the hyper-learning mindset and skillset will prepare us to adapt to change and deliver value in any scenario. Accelerating our learning allows us to determine the questions and answers that will deliver the highest value.

Skeptics may counter that only dedicated time will allow us mastery over a subject. This line of thinking is popularized by the "10,000-hour rule"; in which 10,000 hours of practice will achieve mastery.[2] In actuality, the study that grounds this rule found that both mediocre and elite subjects practiced their craft for the same number of hours. The differentiator was how they practiced.[3] Elite performers achieved their mastery by devoting deliberate hours to honing their skill sets. Elite performers maintained a strict schedule and pushed themselves further in those dedicated hours, without distraction.

How Do You Create Systems to Stay Curious?

As an Individual

Hyper-learning is a specific behavior and approach to productive curiosity that is contingent on growth mindset, which believes we have the potential for growth in all aspects of life. There is always more for us to know and improve upon.

Without productive curiosity, we risk accepting harmful status quo without question. Our brains have evolved to be incredibly efficient, processing 11 million bits of information every second.[4] Only forty of those bits are digested by our conscious mind, with our unconscious mind left to make sense of the rest through a reliance on the familiar, on mental models, and on simple dichotomies. These frequently feed our internal confirmation biases to help us navigate life smoothly. Confirmation bias is the tendency to interpret new evidence as confirmation of one's existing beliefs or theories. When confirmation bias is at play, we often negate the benefit of learning. Imagine you are in a heated debate, so you turn to the Internet's search engine for reassurance. There on the first page, is a link to an article that supports your claim. Just as you go to show it to your counterpart, they present you with the same search query and a different result chosen, this time the resource supports their stance. You likely will have scanned the same titles as each other but have been drawn to the ones that reinforced your existing beliefs. It's a mental shortcut that happens if you do not make the effort to challenge it. This shortcut can result in discriminative biases—the critical importance of preventing these is covered in Chapter 3, "Inclusion and Diversity."

We can perform most day-to-day tasks automatically, and we are conditioned to preserve energy and reduce cognitive load. Human nature has positioned us as creatures of habit. As psychologist Daniel Kahneman puts it, "laziness is built deep into our nature."[5] A fixed mindset believes that this state of being is the endpoint. It shies away from the effort, obstacles, and challenges that disrupt our comfortable habits. Conversely, a growth mindset believes in the value of challenging our natural state, which is crucial to curiosity.

A growth mindset releases us from the constraints of fear and ego nurtured through our schooling and professional lives. We are taught that mistakes have negative consequences, instead of framing them as opportunities for growth. You forget the answers; you will fail the test. You stumble in a presentation; you will be fired. These blunders are valuable insights into where we can focus our energies to improve and highlight where we can explore new approaches.

We are embedded in a rigid system characterized by productivity and success metrics that discourage deviation. Consequently, we avoid ambiguous situations where we are not confident of immediate success because we are overcome by a fear of failure and a loss to our social capital. Although exercises in hyper-learning would bring clarity to those ambiguous situations, it requires a courageous first step to acknowledge, "I don't know." This vulnerability is necessary for curiosity to grow.

> **Reflect:** Has there been a time when the fear of failure prevented you from going after your goals or learning something new?

A growth mindset has been achieved when the following is true:

- You embrace challenges.
- You persist in the face of setbacks.
- You see effort as the path to mastery.
- You learn from criticism.
- You find lessons and inspiration in the success of others.[6]

There are many ways to reframe failure as a positive: fail fast, fail forward, failure is a part of success, the list goes on. Each emphasizes failure as a learning opportunity. It teaches you how to ask the right questions for future endeavors. It teaches you how to be more productively curious. Retrospectives (retros) are a fantastic tool, allowing you to reflect on past failures and find lessons. There are also more immediate ways we can learn and reflect on failure.

One of those methods is saying "Yes, and . . . ." This tool comes from improv comedy, where actors use the phrase to build on one another's jokes. Our team uses it to build on the momentum of one another's ideas. This can happen in an ideation session, or in everyday conversation with our teammates. The word "no" is barred from these creative spaces, fostering a safe environment that removes fear and the desire to protect the ego. It also challenges us to find the benefit and the opportunity in even the worst suggestions put forward, which is often where we can find the most novel solutions. Another way to embrace failure is through the adage, "strong beliefs, loosely held," which encourages us to speak in hypotheses. Framing our statements in hypotheses invites challenge and creates an opportunity to learn and evolve.

Critical to a hyper-learner is realizing when it is necessary to unlearn and relearn. As futurist, author, and advisor, Alvin Toffler once said, "The illiterate of the 21st Century will not be those who cannot read and write, but those who cannot learn, unlearn, and relearn." For example, healthcare providers must keep up with an ever-advancing medical field. Practitioners must learn and incorporate new techniques and also unlearn and relearn best practices within their skillset. This learning cycle is embedded in modern medicine, a field where advances in techniques and technology demand constant learning. This process ensures we are operating at the top of our game: Once something becomes inefficient or ineffective, it is unlearnt and replaced with a more efficient and effective evolution. Staying curious helps us notice when this learning cycle is less embedded or evident.

The COVID-19 global pandemic caused millions to quickly unlearn and relearn how we do things. Socializing with friends and family, where we work, and how we prioritize our time all changed. Everybody was now joining the voices of those who had long been questioning the corporate norms and policies that had been falsely upheld as "the only way." Some teams bonded more virtually than they had in the years of being separated by cubicle walls. Breaking the normal routine for navigating the world created new opportunities to connect.

We can assess other habits and patterns for whether they may contribute to inefficiencies in our lives, work, and teams. Mental models are foundational to understanding our patterns and are a great example for deploying your curiosity to unlearn and relearn at speed. A mental model is any structure through which you understand life and make meaning and can be beneficial or harmful.

A common positive mental model applicable to curiosity is a Forcing Function. A Forcing Function is any task, activity, or event that forces you (and/or your team) to act.[7] They can be set externally (a weekly update meeting), and internally (an arbitrary personal deadline). The importance we attribute to these often-artificial events motivates us to act. This mental model shapes our feelings of accountability by creating time constraints. Other mental models actively hinder efficiency and productivity. Brook's Law describes the belief that adding more people to a project gets it done faster. However, more people can create greater complexity and prolong the project. This is closely tied with the mental model of a "Man Month." A Man Month is a hypothetical unit of work representing the work done by one person in one month. It perpetuates the myth that you can save a month's worth of time by adding a person to a project.

Becoming aware of the negative mental models we subscribe to is necessary to unlearn those and relearn alternative models that increase productivity. The first step is to recognize patterns of mental models at play within your team. Why not work as a team to research some of these models and use the hyper-learning framework below to share your learnings?

> **Reflect:** What mental models do you want your team to unlearn and relearn?

Rapid unlearning-relearning is also helpful when working with different clients. A successful approach with one client does not guarantee the same results with another. It is important to balance between viewing every client engagement as unique and leveraging established best practices. Staying productively curious will help achieve this equilibrium. When faced with new situations, it is crucial to understand what and how much you need to know to thrive. Here, I take inspiration from

Colin Powell, the former Secretary of State, and his famous 40–70 decision-making principle. Powell's 40–70 rule states that you should strive to understand between 40 and 70 percent of the available information before making a decision. Less than 40 percent, you are under- or misinformed. More than 70 percent, you have likely lost the differentiating instinctive edge to your judgment, or worse, the moment for impactful decision-making has completely passed. Hyper-learning allows you to achieve that 40 to 70 percent of information at a speed that will give you a competitive edge.

As a Team

On my second day on the team, I joined an ongoing virtual session with twenty participants. I came in mid-project with new teammates, a new topic area, and new tools. It was the ultimate experiential learning and helped me internalize the team's mantra: play in the grey. It was also an efficient way to address my many curiosities as a new team member.

Learning from experience is a form of discovery learning and an inductive way to acquire knowledge. The process is more meaningful for knowledge internalization, retention, and application than receptive learning. Unfortunately, accumulating a comprehensive set of knowledge and skills for a professional role through experience and discovery learning alone is inefficient and time-consuming. A diverse team of members who stay curious through hyper-learning becomes a significant asset to the team. Imagine if their accumulated years of wisdom and experience could be internalized by a new hire in under ninety days.

The action-orientated element of productive curiosity and hyper-learning promotes more meaningful learning than a receptive learning technique or wandering through information. The learner must memorize the information and understand in order to deploy it at the relevant moment.

This knowledge transfer can only take place when the whole team stays curious. Full team engagement through retros is a fantastic hyper-learning opportunity to share an individual's discovery with the broader team. A retro is a specific meeting time to regularly reflect on work and find opportunities for improvement. These meetings are often triggered by specific events—the end of a client engagement, a product delivered to market, or a completed presentation. The individuals directly involved with the work will chart how it went against the expected path of execution, identifying what went well, what didn't, and other areas to explore. To succinctly share experiential learnings, an individual must have internalized their own reflections. The presentation, discussion, and Q&A compound the learning for the individual and benefit the team.

Many enterprises have a wealth of training and development resources available through their company wide intranets. If nobody has the time or incentive to use them, they deliver little value. A new hire may acquaint themselves with a few of these at the start of a new role, but their day-to-day tasks will increase and take precedence. Professional education to the bottom of the "to-do" list. The best teams don't let this happen because they understand the importance of staying curious to consistently deliver value.

Reflect: How will you make an ongoing commitment to learning and staying curious?

Everyone has interests and passions that influence what they choose to learn. That's why staying curious is a team endeavor. When each individual is incentivized to synthesize and share their diverse learnings with their teammates, value, and impact are multiplied.

A team can prioritize learning by creating space for it. We need to abide by the theory of spaced repetition to cement the information in our long-term memory. Spaced repetition is scientifically proven to improve efficient learning. It posits that the optimum time to test yourself on new information is just before you are about to forget it. As this process is repeated, the forgetting curve becomes shallower, as seen in Figure 5.1.[8] The result is that information needs to be retested less frequently, from every to once a year. A team that implements this concept helps new hires achieve rapid success.

Cultivating hyper-learning can be done through:

1. Low-pressure testing environments with judgment-free feedback
2. Space for discussion
3. Opportunities to share

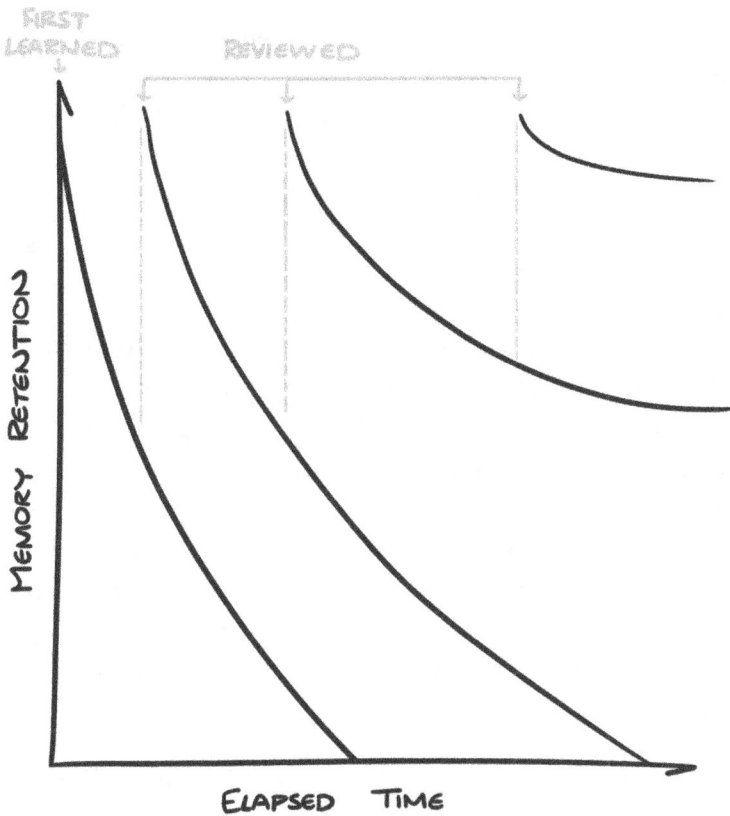

Figure 5.1 Spaced repetition eases the forgetting curve

Low-Pressure Testing Environments With Judgment-Free Feedback

One way for a team to create action around spaced repetition is to orchestrate low-pressure testing environments. To remove fear and damage to the ego, it is necessary to frame these as tests against yourself, not others. As design thinkers, the Fusion team has a selection of core frameworks that every team member needs to be well-versed in and able to present in a unified, consistent way. Experienced team members teach these to the newer hires, and a "challenge" follows over a period of time. The challenge is a free-for-all where team members call upon one another to present a specific framework at any unexpected point of the day. It's a rapid 5-minute exercise where one presents and the other provides feedback through the

"Keepers and Improvers" structure.[9] Keepers and Improvers is a method that gives feedback in threes: three aspects that went well and should be continued, and three aspects that could change to make next time better. The process continues until everyone is comfortable and proficient with the new frameworks. Those who have been on the team longer have shallower forgetting curves, so this challenge offers them a helpful refresher.

Space for Discussion

Another way the team can prioritize hyper-learning is to create space for discussion. The ability to discuss and explain a subject is crucial to internalizing information. Simon Sinek draws the comparison to school: Which classroom did you work hardest and strive to learn in? Was it the one that you felt truly engaged and able to contribute, or where you only absorbed knowledge?[10] As a geographically dispersed team, we are intentional about conducting discussions that may otherwise occur impromptu at a workspace. One strategy is to dedicate space on your communication platform to share new and inspiring findings that can potentially accelerate the whole team.

Opportunities to Share

A great team attracts people with diverse passions. Personal interests have a positive impact on the individual's professional life by providing additional context and ways of thinking. A team that prioritizes staying curious also understands the power of sharing extra-curricular interests with each other. Creating a dedicated space like a casual presentation or Q&A, allows the presenter to develop or flex their hyper-learning skills by synthesizing their experience and sharing it with novices. The audience rapidly consumes information and consolidates it through active discussion, perhaps inspiring new passions of their own.

What Does Staying Curious Look Like?

Fulfilling productive curiosity looks different for every individual, depending on their learning style and needs. Regardless of our personal approach to learning, a focused balance of time and attention is usually required to maximize its effectiveness. These are two finite resources that are frequent constraints for professional progress and need proactive time management. Deep Work and the Pomodoro Method are two recommended techniques to enable hyper-learning.[11]

Deep Work, outlined by Cal Newport, is a method to amplify productivity. High productivity is the result of time spent multiplied by the intensity of focus. For many of us, intense focus is easily eroded by multi tasking or digital distractions. Deep Work entails immersing yourself in distraction-free work for an extended period. This zone of productivity is the ideal setting to learn at speed. Newport defines three core steps to a Deep Work zone:

1. **Schedule Deep Work:** Placing a calendar hold on your schedule will signal to others that this is a time for deep uninterrupted work. A team that supports hyper-learning will understand and respect the importance of this.
2. **Create Physical Space:** Go to a quiet room to separate yourself from distractions. If you are in an office, wear headphones to signal that you are immersing yourself in a task.
3. **Create Digital Space:** Close your e-mail and any other online distractions and notifications that may disrupt your mindset to avoid time wasted on context switching.

Once you have created dedicated space and time for Deep Work, Francesco Cirillo's Pomodoro Method can be implemented. The Pomodoro Method enhances your ability to focus and respects your finite time and attention by enabling you to get more done in a shorter timeframe. Use an analog timer to minimize digital distraction and follow these steps:

1. Choose what you are going to learn.
2. Set a timer for 25 minutes.
3. Work until that timer is done.
4. Take a few minutes break.
5. Repeat until you have been working for 90 minutes.
6. Take a longer break.

How you learn during these sessions varies for each individual, and it is worth taking the time to discover your own optimal technique. For example, as someone who is a reading/writing learner, I like to follow Mortimer Adler's guidance on How to Read a Book.[12] There are different ways to read a book, and each book should be given only the amount of time that it deserves. Inspectional reading is the art of reading to get the most out of a book in a given time and is ideal for hyper-learning on a given subject. By following the Inspectional Reading approach, below, you'll be primed with the book's overall content framework, which will shape how you'll read the book:

1. **Find:** Find a list of what looks like the top books in the field.
2. **Filter:** Filter the top five books by top recommendations or 4.5+ star reviews.
3. **Inspect:** Inspect the contents of each book by reading the chapter headings and the last page of each chapter.
4. **Digest:** Only if it seems worth it, digest the contents by spending more time to take notes and question how it relates to what you already know.

Action is what truly underpins all styles of hyper-learning. Without a bias toward action, learners may fall prey to the illusion of fluency. The illusion of fluency is the belief that being able to easily repeat something constitutes learning it.[13] Learning is not useful in a work environment unless it is actionable. The ability to apply new knowledge to appropriate scenarios is evidence of having a truly deep understanding. There are several active learning strategies you can experiment with. Peter Brown's *Make It Stick* offers a good place to start:[14]

1. **Elaborate:** Synthesize and expand on the learned concept and then share it with somebody else using your own materials.
2. **Generate:** Recall the information without looking at reference material. Even imperfect recall is better for memory building than looking at the information without attempting to recall it.

3. **Calibrate:** In addition to the team challenges discussed above, independently quiz yourself with low stakes. This provides an objective measure of whether you know the material or not.

4. **Reflect:** Review your learning experience to cement the learning and identify what you should iterate on next time.

The Make it Stick technique is effective for designing and delivering point-of-view (POV) presentations. A POV is an example of thought leadership and a means of propelling your team to the next level. It is a beautifully presented and well-researched stance on a timely topic or trend that can be shared as a value-add and accelerator throughout your organization. It is a product of hyper-learning. Steps 1 through 3 of Make it Stick will prepare you to present and field Q&A on your POV.

According to business theorist Arie de Geus, "The ability to learn faster than competitors may be the only sustainable competitive advantage."[15] A wealth of information is out there; the differentiator is who can access what is most relevant and do something meaningful with it the quickest. Productive curiosity engages critical thinking, communication, collaboration, and creativity. It is a critical trait to foster within yourself and your team to ignite a new level of learning and ability to deliver high-value impact.

Key Takeaways

Take an Online Quiz to Assess Your Growth Mindset

Check out resources like the London Academy of IT: www.londonacademyofit.co.uk/blog/interactive-quiz-fixed-vs-growth-mindset. Once you know where you are on the journey to a growth mindset, you can identify new ways to push your thinking and stay curious.

Create Team and Individual Systems to Celebrate Productive Curiosity

Start a new team ritual of scheduling deep work time on your calendars at the beginning of each week. Alternate these between individual time and cooperative low-pressure testing time. Ensure these blocks of time are protected and respected.

Discover Your Preferred Learning Method and Work to Make It Hyper

Talk to colleagues to learn about different learning styles or take an online quiz to find out if you are a visual, auditory, reading/writing, or kinetic learner.

Use the resources referenced in this chapter as a starting point to find hyper-learning methods that accelerate you.

CHAPTER 6

Artists and Scientists

By Jacob Colling

Niklas Luhmann, a German sociologist and general thinker, is credited as being one of the most important sociologists of the 20th century. Luhmann wrote 70 books and over 400 scholarly articles during his career. He had a unique system for growing his knowledge over time called the "slip box." He described it as something he could have a conversation with. At the core of it, Luhmann had developed a process and repeatable pattern for digesting interesting information and making it available for his future self. You can do the same, and if you combine a few other best practices from the most prolific artists and scientists, such as identifying your own creative lineage and working in public, you'll also be able to out-produce your peers. Improving your workflow will enable you to produce the most you can, and therefore, produce your best work.

The most important factor that ensures you are headed in the right direction is knowing your WHY. Once you are confident in your direction, figure out how to get there more effectively.

In this chapter, we'll walk through the entire process of transforming inspiration into work, sharing that work in public, and engaging in a community of creators.

Finding Inspiration in Your Creative Lineage

Creative Lineage

Staring at a blank sheet of paper or an empty canvas can be intimidating. Deciding you want to make something but not knowing how or not having inspiration amplifies that feeling. Start by identifying your creative lineage. This is a family tree of creators, writers, artists, and craftspeople who have inspired you. Then, build that lineage by diving deeply into their work. Look at all their paintings, understand who their contemporaries were, read their journals, and piece together their place in the world. In that process, you'll likely discover who inspired that artist. You can then repeat the process to understand where their inspiration came from. Repeat. By studying your inspiration and their inspiration, you'll grow your creative lineage. You're now standing on the shoulders of generations of creators who have stood in the same spot as you. Creating can often be a lonely process, but there is less to fear when you have such inspiring mentors.

For more contemporary members of your creative lineage, there are resources like podcasts, YouTube videos, and documentaries. You might even be able to find courses that they've taught. Aspiring fantasy novelists can listen to N. K. Jemisin on the Ezra Klein Podcast[1] give a free master class in world-building as the first author to win the Hugo Award for Best Novel in three consecutive years, as well as the first to win for all three novels in a trilogy. For a more detailed tutorial, the author has her own course on the learning platform MasterClass.

Example

Throughout each step, I'll walk you through how I've applied these learnings as a nontechnical person learning how to code and developing the skillset to build a web application.

Through social media and community websites, I stumbled on a group of people who founded small businesses with their software development skillsets. These individuals made small micro-products serving small niches, often making reasonable profits as the only person in their business. I didn't have the skill set to become a software engineer at a big tech company, but I thought I could make a micro-product. I had found my inspiration and formed a virtual community around me as I learned from each of their journeys.

Idea Generation

In science, it's quite apparent that every breakthrough is built on citations to other scientists. With artists, it's less tangible, but every artist has been inspired by someone who led them through their craft. This means that you are never creating alone. Others' ideas are with you, whether at the forefront or in the back of your mind. Regardless of where they reside, they can be a source of inspiration.

A blank canvas or sheet of paper can thwart inspiration. Instead, collect and digest raw materials before you sit down to work. Collecting inspiration happens differently depending on the craft, but the steps are the same:

- Spend time regularly exploring others' work.
- Capture and save the work that speaks to you.
- Make it your own.

Let's take writing as an example to illustrate this. Aspiring writers start by being readers. They read anything that inspires them, from literature to newspapers. They do not consume passively. When a sentence has a unique rhythm to it or has a clever play on words, they collect that sentence. They highlight it and mark it as a source for future inspiration or learning.

The real value comes from making an idea your own. If it's a nonfiction highlight, that means rearticulating the main idea in your own words. For fiction, it might be jotting down what emotion the sentence evoked and reflecting on how you might do something similar.

This type of reading is slow because it's deliberate. Deliberate learning is highly effective for integrating new ideas and inspiration into your knowledge base. Master Sommeliers don't chug a glass of wine when they are tasting it. The only way to speed up this process is to make it repeatable. That is why it's so critical to build a workflow, which we will get to in the next section, but first, a warning about the pitfalls of collecting content.

> **Reflect**: Who is in your creative lineage? How do you consume their work?

Creators Beware

You need baseline information to create something, so you should read papers, watch movies, or look at paintings; whatever is relevant to your craft. The trap people fall into is consuming without producing., When you feel the need to continue researching, discovering, and finding information, consuming can be a form of procrastination. A less extreme version is to collect information for the sake of collecting. Read-later applications enable you to save an article with the click of a button and even sync it automatically to your preferred note-taking application. For the visual creators, image-driven social media sites and platforms for sharing designs offer the same utility. These platforms make it seamless to save inspiration for later. However, if you never use it later, it won't do you any good. Even businesspeople are susceptible to this. A budding entrepreneur might research different industries and business models, but it doesn't move them closer to launching their business.

> **Reflect:** Look back on your calendar for the last week or month. What percentage of time did you spend creating? Now, how much time did you spend researching? What is the ratio between the two?

There is no perfect ratio for creating versus consuming. It will vary for each project and for each individual's maturity in their craft. However, if you are consistently researching more than you are creating, you might want to take a fresh look at how you are spending your time.

The best way to make your research investment more productive is to make it more usable. It's important to establish a workflow for processing these ideas as you encounter them. That way, you aren't a collector of inspiration but truly an inspired artist.

Your Workflow

The shipping container revolutionized shipping and global logistics. Before containers, every individual item or package being shipped stood alone on its own pallet. Loading and unloading a ship took forever because each item had to be handled individually. Once everything was loaded onto the ship, there was a ton of leftover space that wasn't being used.

The container revolutionized this by packaging individual items into containers. By packaging everything into a uniform shape, it transformed logistics. Now all the longshoremen loading the ships can work with a uniformly sized object. Instead of each unique item requiring analysis and planning to load it on the ship, they can operate efficiently with the same 20-foot container.

On the ship itself, space is used more effectively because the containers are stackable and interlocking. There is still some empty space in the containers themselves, but the overall empty space is reduced by an order of magnitude.

The parallel to knowledge or creative work is clear. Without a process or workflow, we must process each idea or task uniquely and from scratch. We are the logistics people prior to shipping containers. If we create a workflow that is consistent, we'll see a personal transformation, similar to the global logistics transformation. For fans of David Allen's *Getting Things Done*,[2] or Sörnke Ahrens' *How to Take Smart Notes*[3] (which happens to be about Niklas Luhmann's slip box method), this should sound familiar. They are all grounded in the same cognitive principles.

Containerizing Your Ideas or Inspiration as a Simple Three-Step Process

1. **Atomize:** Break down the idea into its smallest standalone parts.
2. **Tag:** Label it such that you can easily discover it later when you need it.
3. **Structure:** Apply whatever the required structure for that container is. You'll have to create these structures based on your craft.

Atomize sounds intuitive, but it's not the same as breaking a project down into separate tasks. If it's an idea, inspiration, or learning, atomic means the smallest possible version of the idea but with all the context needed to understand it. You shouldn't have to look elsewhere in your notes to understand.

Tagging is as straightforward as it sounds. Label the container with all the information you need to find it later. You should optimize for discovery. Ask yourself, "Under what context do I want to find this later?" If you are collecting and digesting new raw material, you will eventually forget a lot of it. Therefore, making it discoverable in your personal system is essential to resurfacing it later.

Structure is the consistent framing you use for a given type of idea. It will vary depending on what you are containerizing. A journal entry might be packaged differently than inspiration or a key learning. It also varies with your personal style. What are you trying to accomplish by saving that article or studying that song? Think about the goal you are working toward. Based on that, what do you need out of these items?

Below are a few examples of different container structures:

- New ideas coming in
- Documenting to-dos
- Learnings/Mistakes
- Things you want to learn in the future
- Summaries of key articles

Customize and implement these three practices to containerize ideas or inspirations as they strike. As you build out your workflow, spend time exploring different modalities. Do you prefer electronic notes or a notebook? Does your craft require a sketchbook instead? I won't pronounce any system as the best here because that will depend completely on your context. I personally use electronic notes and a browser-based tool. If you search "best notetaking apps" plus the current year, I'm sure you'll find a suitable list for text-based systems.

Example

In my coding journey, I constantly run into roadblocks while building something. Once I solve that roadblock, I tend to run into it again later. I've learned to document key learnings or silly mistakes to avoid them in the future. For both, I use the same structure.

Atomize: I write down where and what I was working on and include snippets of the code to demonstrate. I also include a link to relevant sources that helped me move past the block. When I review these in the future, everything is self-contained.

Tag: I tag them as "Key Learning" or "Silly Mistake," depending on if I need to learn something or fix a mistake I created. I also include the relevant area. It might be "Backend Database" or "Display Tables." These are one level above the problem area to make them easy to find. If I run into a problem with my database later, I can search "Database" in my notes and find all the challenges I've run into alongside my solutions.

Structure: I keep three bullet points for each container, and they are always the same. The discipline to complete these in sufficient detail is the crux of the whole system:

- Problem/Question—What was I trying to do or solve?
- Solution—What finally worked. I always include a snippet of the functioning code here, so I can come back to it and see an example in my own words.
- Source—What led me in the right direction? Normally this is a link to Stack Overflow or a similar website where people ask questions about coding.

The magic of the system is that I've done all the thinking upfront. Now I have an easy process to document my learnings, making it easier for me to revisit problems and solutions in the future.

Playing Scales

There is a common misconception that everything you publish or produce must be perfect. That's simply not true. In fact, most of the greats across all fields of study or art got there because they simply produced the most. Thinking back to Niklas Luhmann, he was probably a bright individual, but publishing more books than anyone else got him very far. Simply put, quantity begets quality. You want to be intentional about it.

One of the ways to get more reps in than anyone else is to have a repeatable practice you can do for a specific part of your craft. Pianists practice the fundamentals of their art by playing scales. It's something they can do to warm up as well as to stay sharp. Finding your equivalent and playing scales frequently is important.

Some of the creative individuals I know do different types of sketches to keep their skills sharp. One of their "playing scales" exercises is sketching their own hand, with a pencil in their drawing hand, a nondominant hand on the table, and a piece of paper. The hand has so many rich details and challenging proportions that it's impossible to get perfect. They can easily replicate this exercise wherever they go. Those same people also do sketches during their morning meetings. It helps them process information and, incidentally, they get another 1–2 sketches per day. When there are on average 255 workdays per year, those daily sketches add up. Without doing any other type of practice, they've done 500+ sketches over the year. Skill compounds over time and an extra 500 reps per year make a difference.

Perhaps my favorite "playing scales" example, is a repeatable practice used to hone writing skills by applying what John McPhee, author of 30+ books and the writing mentor of many modern-day greats, called "greening."[4] The practice arose from newspaper editors who had limited printing space and needed to trim articles further. The writer takes a draft of an article and highlights in green the words or sentences that can be removed to make that section more concise. The writers were told to use green in case the section could be left in, which was almost never the case. It served practical purposes but is also the perfect way to practice the writing maxim "omit needless words." Writers can apply this to their own drafts or test their pen against their favorite authors.

Creating a structured and repeatable process that increases reps enables you to practice more. Incorporate this type of practice with your system for containerizing ideas and your skill will naturally compound over time.

Example

Engineers and software developers have numerous online programs to test their skills in the form of daily coding challenges. I'm not skilled enough to call myself a developer yet, but I have started doing coding challenges. An example of an easy challenge is: determine if a given word is a palindrome. It takes 10–20 minutes for someone like me to code a program to do that. Reading through the recommended solution afterward helps me learn how to write better code.

Working in Public

The final principle to becoming prolific is to work in public. This means sharing your ups and downs, your drafts and finished products, your questions, and eventual answers. It might sound intimidating, but this principle holds everything else together. You'll end up meeting like-minded people, getting feedback that elevates your craft, and once you start, it will keep you accountable.

Meeting like-minded people will help you get better simply through your interactions. You're not guaranteed to get a big break and become famous, but you can count on incrementally building a community or discovering an existing one. Your community will become a source of inspiration and accountability. You'll meet people who are in the same position as you or have recently been. They'll be able to offer insight informed by their own journey.

When you work in public, you'll meet critics. Some of them are helpful, but many are not. Listen to the helpful ones and ignore the rest. As Adam Grant details in his book *Originals*, the people best positioned to evaluate an idea are experts in that field. If a layperson is bashing your artwork, you're likely safe to ignore them. If someone you respect in the field is providing criticism, you might want to incorporate it.[5]

In addition to working in public, more people are publishing raw or unpolished content. You can see this in the indie game development community by searching for the hashtag #screenshotsaturday on Twitter. Every Saturday across the indie game development community, individuals share screenshots of their work in progress. It can be good encouragement to keep producing when you know people will see your #screenshotsaturday.

The benefits of working in public are immense and compound when you regularly share and engage with your community. Developing the muscle to work in public is a keystone habit that propels all your creative endeavors. You'll be supported during your low times and will have people to celebrate your wins.

Example

My journey of working in public is just starting it has already been extremely productive. I've connected with creators I respect and started relationships with investors. I've learned about new tools I never would have found otherwise. One person shared the source code of their product with me so I could borrow one of his internal tools.

This isn't a magic bullet, and it won't work for you right away. I've personally picked up different coding projects at least four different times over the last 6–7 years. I've dabbled a lot, but it never stuck. I'd try something, make progress, and then get stuck. I'd stop working on it. A year later I'd try again. I'd forget what I learned and start again from square one. Over time those loose collections of learnings have accumulated into something meaningful. Now that I'm putting a process and structure around my learning, I've gained tremendous momentum.

I hope that by sharing this with you, you will be able to skip those years of starting and stopping projects. I hope you can start with a solid foundation and build momentum quickly. Having a system in place from the beginning, and allowing it to evolve, will remove a lot of friction. With that friction gone, you can create more, go faster, and go further!

Key Takeaways

Create Your Creative Lineage

Grab a sheet of paper. List out your favorite creators across all genres— artists, musicians, businesspeople, scientists. List them all.

Now pick three. One at a time, Google "Who inspired [name you wrote down]." Skim a few articles and find who inspired your inspiration. Write them down and draw connecting lines on your paper.

You have the first branches of your creative family tree!

Play Your Scales

What is the most basic building block of what you do? Once you've identified that, go a layer deeper. What's even more granular? Write it out. Find the most repeatable way to practice your craft. Schedule time to get back to the basics and just practice.

Identify Your Workflow

In the proceeding step, you've identified the granular components of your craft. Now that you've done that, work through the Atomize, Tag, Structure framework and identify what each of those steps looks like for your craft. Then, go through a single real-life example and make it real.

Work in Public

Take your latest creation and share it. It doesn't matter what platform it's on or if it's you just walking a friend through your work. It's okay if this is intimidating. It is for everyone. Just share one thing at a time and keep doing it. Once you've made your post, find someone in your community, and show support for them. Make sure you do this second, though, so you don't procrastinate on sharing your own work first!

PART 2

Empowering Teams

The Buddy System

By Lianza Reyes

you learn to accept the scraped knees
and instead keep your head to face the breeze,
you learn, instead, to look to your companion,
and acknowledge that your teamwork will reign champion.
the bruises mean little if you still run together
in fact, they remind that you achieve under pressure.
clasped hands, never commanding the other,
equals kindly challenging to go even farther
you must know the buddy system at times will take patience
but in the end, you hand them applause with no hesitation,
the going gets tough, and then, it'll get tougher,
yet there's no one who helps you more than coworkers
even if things are way harder than what it seems,
these all lighten up when you are *empowering your team.*

CHAPTER 7

Intentional Communication

By Patrick Hanley

Communication is a special thing; some would go the distance and say it is magical. The magic lies in the connections you can build with any living thing around you; humans (friends, partners, baristas), animals, and even nature, by coexisting with your surroundings. You can bring this same energy to your team and build those bonds with one another on a deeper level. According to a report published by McKinsey, knowledge workers spend an average of 14 percent of their workweek communicating and collaborating internally. The study also showed that improving internal collaboration through social tools could help raise the productivity of interaction by as much as 20 to 25 percent.[1]

Intentional communication can be cultivated and leveraged to build a high-performance team. We've found a combination of communication tools, techniques, and mindsets that spark significant growth in intentional communication. First, by building trust, accountability, and psychological safety you can open the span of possibilities for your team's potential. Second, by employing ritual design you can generate specific behaviors, words, and actions which reinforce your goals, values, and performance objectives.

Communicating to Build Trust

It takes everyone's involvement to make a team great and being great is easier when you have a team supporting you and rooting for you to succeed. Imagine there was a way to build a system within your team that would enable everyone to encourage everyone—powerful huh?

To build that system, we must hold ourselves accountable to agreed-upon expectations of communication and actions. Holding oneself accountable builds trust amongst teammates, yet can often be difficult to foster. According to Monday.com,

> 91 percent of employees feel that accountability is one of the most important things they'd like to see in their workplace. 82 percent of those same respondents felt that they have no power to hold anyone accountable in the workplace.[2]

The manner by which you can build a virtuous cycle of accountability and trust is by putting in the work of cultivating psychological safety, openness to feedback, and an environment of transparency.

Psychological Safety

First, work to create an environment of psychological safety where every individual feels comfortable sharing ideas, speaking their minds, and doing their job without the fear of judgment or ridicule. As your team members feel accepted and respected, deeper levels of communication can occur. Psychological safety is not a milestone, it's a continuous journey that must be worked on every day by everyone on the team.

Feedback

You will read the importance of feedback many times in this book. Feedback grows most readily out of safe environments where individuals know that the feedback being shared comes from the heart. It is important to approach feedback in a meaningful way that is helpful and not hurtful.

Transparency

Transparency can grow on a foundation of psychological safety and feedback. It is an essential outcome because great teams *need* to be able to communicate freely and effectively with each other. Environments where important information cannot be shared because trust doesn't exist stifle a team's ability to achieve greatness.

Ritual Design

Our team has formed deeply connected bonds and collaboration through the practice of ritual design. Rituals evoke common meaning, consistency, reliability, and trust. Ritual design is the act of intentionally creating moments of connection and meaning between individuals that express specific intentions, support values, and create connectivity between teammates. In the course of roughly two weeks, we observed the usage of over 100 rituals in use on our team. Some were small, such as saying, "Yes, and . . ." to a teammate's idea. Some were much more in-depth, such as a retrospective on a recent client engagement.

As a primer for how to incorporate ritual design into your team's performance, we can think of ritual design in three phases: discovery, design, and live. In *discovery*, we focus on what is important to us as a team—goals, impact, principles, and values. Once clearly identified, we can begin to *design* the ritual that reinforces that goal, the achievement of impact, or the expression of our values. These rituals, per the example above, can be simple phrases, shared gestures like a high-five, or highlighting a win at specific times during the week. The simpler the design the better, as simplicity fuels action. The final phase is where we *live* our rituals. This is where the power of ritual design emerges as it takes hold in your team and the verbal, nonverbal, patterned, and consistent behaviors that reinforce your team's mission are visible every day.

To expand this learning, in the following paragraphs, we'll share how we've cultivated ritual design on our team to ensure we're communicating intentionally and performing to our team's agreed-upon standards. We break down our communication and rituals into three categories:

1. Whole team
2. Individual, but together
3. Bonding

Whole Team

Whole team rituals are things we intend to do together, for the purpose of full team alignment and contribution. Below are some examples of whole team rituals we practice:

- **Blueprinting:** Our team blueprint is our secret sauce to operational success. It is the scroll that we unroll and refer to when we are doing our primary form of work. It enables all team members to understand what we do and how we do it. It contains steps, tips, and dos and don'ts, to set every team member up for success. You may be thinking, who created this blueprint? Who is in charge of it? The answer is, everyone on the team. We have designed a ritual of blueprinting our work, our learning, and our process enhancements. We dedicate time every month to update it as a full team and discuss additions we want to make. This is a highly important ritual designed specifically to apply continuous improvement to the foundation of our operations. It ensures everyone's learning contributes to our team's success. Blueprinting binds our team to our operating model. More on this in Chapter 8, "Value Blueprinting."
- **Project Retrospectives:** Retrospectives are a critical ritual in support of how we analyze and evolve our craft. These post-project reviews enable the entire team to understand what was done, what worked, and what we learned, to improve our delivery at the next opportunity. Retrospectives also inform blueprinting—these rituals go hand in hand. Retrospectives are a ritual because they are intentional and consistent. The team knows when, where, and how key learnings will be disseminated, and that builds trust as well as attentiveness to performance.
- **Standup:** Our daily Standup meetings are highly ritualized by design. It is how and when we run our business. Each day assumes a specific focus by which everyone on the team knows what will be discussed, when certain questions will be answered, and when specific updates will be shared. Within these daily rituals, we incorporate rituals that also allow individuals to bring their whole selves to work. Our daily stand-up rituals are:
- **Monday:** Recap of weekend activities and work priorities for the week ahead
- **Tuesday:** Leadership "mindreading" on what everyone needs to know strategically

- **Wednesday:** Full pipeline and project review
- **Thursday:** Learning and training
- **Friday:** Visual demonstration of what was delivered

Individual, but Together

These are rituals that focus on personal growth and progress. To accelerate growth and performance, we place a high value on seeking and giving feedback. Setting the right parameters helps everyone understand how to give feedback in a meaningful way to achieve a better outcome. Below are some examples of *individual, but together* rituals we practice:

- **Monthly Reflection:** According to one report, *"70 percent of employees would feel better about themselves if their boss were more grateful."*[3] The central method we use to promote gratitude, as well as personal and team growth, is monthly reflection. Our ritual is a monthly meeting where we come together to share what we're grateful for about each teammate, and what we can do to improve performance as a team. This ritual encourages us to think specifically about the good each teammate brings to the team and recognize how each one of us has played a crucial role in that success. We end our monthly reflection with an open discussion on how we can improve the team. Keeping our feedback on "improvers" at the team—as opposed to the individual level—creates a nonthreatening environment for improvement and empowers team members to tackle opportunities to elevate our team.

- **Wins:** Celebrating wins on our team is a beloved ritual. When a teammate achieves greatness by completing a project, steps out of their comfort zones, and achieves a milestone—no matter how big or small—we recognize them publicly and celebrate with them. The person who shares the win may be a teammate working on a project with the individual being recognized or may have just witnessed someone on the team accomplish great things. This ritual ensures we're celebrating successes and also actively looking for the successes of others.

Bonding

Bonding is critically important for the psychological safety of the team. By taking extra time in the short term, you will create an environment that is ultimately productive in the long run. Below are some examples of bonding rituals we practice:

- **One-on-Ones:** We prioritize one-on-one meetings on the team and encourage it for new hires too. Scheduling one-on-ones is integrated into their first 90-day action plan and has multiple benefits. The team gets to know the new contributor, and the new team member reduces the anxiety of how to reach out to members of the team. As an intentional ritual, team members can gather new ideas, connect interpersonally, and share insights on projects with other team members.

- **Personal Highlights:** Personal highlights are shared during our Monday and Friday stand-ups. On Mondays, we share a highlight from the weekend, and on Fridays, we share a personal highlight from the week. This takes less than 30 seconds per person and shines a personal light on families, hobbies, goals, accomplishments, and so much more. We learn who people are and the depth of their backgrounds and interests.

Connecting deeply as a team can only be achieved when bonds are formed throughout the day, week, month, or year. The rituals a team creates and sustains are a part of what defines the uniqueness of a team and transforms them from merely a group of people into a connected and purposeful team. When I interviewed to join as a designer, the interview experience signaled that this was going to be an entirely different kind of team I'd be joining. For example, beginning each interview section by sharing where we are on the Mood Elevator to build empathy for one another, and concluding interview sections with Keepers and Improvers[4] to reinforce team values of having a growth mindset and viewing feedback is a gift. In retrospect, I now know the thought, purpose, and deliberate nature behind every ritual I experienced during my interview.

> **Reflect:** What rituals do you already have on your team that enable intentional communication? Are they driving specific results?

Establishing your own team rituals and creating intentional practices around communicating within your team allows for cross-team accountability and trust. We've shared some of the methods we use to push our team's boundaries of effective communication, establish meaningful rituals, and create space for whole-team and individual contributions. Now, it's your turn to put these ideas into action!

Key Takeaways

Communicate With Intent

Be intentional with your communication system. It should be by design.

Foster Psychological Safety

Hold yourself and your team accountable to build and maintain a psychologically safe space for your team to give feedback, promote transparency, and build trust.

Discover, Define, and Live Your Rituals

Understand the rituals that exist, and what rituals you would like to implement on your team to reinforce behaviors and communication that drive you toward your goals and speak your values.

CHAPTER 8

Value Blueprinting

By Haya Alzaid López

Restaurant staff meet daily to recap yesterday's service, review the menu in detail, and provide feedback on the previous day's performance. This is how their teams work so intricately together while evolving their menu, plating design, operational efficiencies, and overall dining experience. This enables a consistent and remarkable experience for all customers while creating space for elements to surprise and delight.

Building a blueprint is critical to any team's success. It paves the way to determining where in your process you exhibit your team's values and how you deliberately drive toward that mission through your work. There are a variety of strategic and roadmap-based blueprints that exist. In this chapter, we will focus on value blueprints.

Blueprinting Your Way to Success

When our team built our first value blueprint, we had a proven business model we had fine-tuned over several years. Our blueprinting process was about finding a way to articulate our full end-to-end process and identify our most essential best practices that differentiate our work. We also wanted to avoid unnecessary repeat learnings where possible, meaning two people going through the same experimentation and arriving at the same outcome.

Value blueprints ensure you have reinforceable processes in place that reflect the value you provide your customers. Value blueprinting is an ongoing, iterative process of identifying experiments and fine-tuning best practices.

The blueprinting process is critical because it is a path to explicitly identify where in your process you exhibit your team's values and mission. For example, your team may strive to be adaptable and flexible to customer needs, but that goal needs to be reinforced with strategic processes and tools. To find your team's unique, value-based differentiator, blueprint your work by following this simple and iterative process.

The four essential steps to crafting your team's blueprint:

1. Build your foundation for future simplicity.
2. Deploy your blueprint for increased performance.
3. Experiment with big and small to grow.
4. Reflect, evolve, repeat.

> **Reflect:** In what ways does your team add value to others? How might you create a process around that value to ensure it maintains consistency?

Blueprinting is building a thoughtful approach to processes, experiments, and evolutions. All teams can benefit from establishing a deep understanding of the intricacies within their process, regardless of a product or service focus.

For product-based teams, the blueprinting process allows you to map everything, from how you interact with prospective or long-term clients to how you manage hiring and onboarding. Product-based teams can also blueprint the critical pieces that contribute to the ongoing success of that product. However, just mapping out the workflows and processes isn't enough. Taking a blueprinting approach allows your team to review your operations in a way that allows you to go deep into the details and potentially identify opportunities to work differently and drive further innovation.

Many service-based companies struggle to both identify and communicate how their offering is unique compared to others in the market. In very simple terms, everyone's offering is unique because of the nature of the team's make-up and the ideas contributed. However, there must be deliberate thought and specialized attention placed on the actual process or methodology of how that team generates incredible work and remains competitive.

Regardless of whether you're primarily a product or a service-based company or team, there are a variety of different contexts you can blueprint, including:

1. Your core offerings
2. All your products and/or services
3. Your team's operating system and how work gets done
4. Your team's hiring and onboarding process (more about this in Chapter 11, "Team Growth and Expansion")

This chapter, and much of this book, will guide you on how to ask yourself the hard questions, think deeply about your own processes, and align them to your team's desired outcomes.

To achieve success in this process, be prepared to conduct a detailed analysis of your team's work, balanced with an empathy-based assessment of your customers' needs. Throughout this process, you will discover your team's unique abilities while ensuring you meet your customer's core needs.

Build Your Foundation for Future Simplicity

Technology on our team evolves rapidly. We don't shy away from shifting from one file management tool to a different one or shifting from one team chat tool to another. Sometimes it's self-imposed by the team, and sometimes it's imposed by our company. Regardless of the type of technology or tool shift, our core work is not disrupted because the foundation we built for how we work as a team is proven and constant.

To lay the groundwork for your blueprint, you must account for the people, the processes, and the technology that fuels your work to deliver value.

People

Define one or two people to lead the blueprint process holistically. This should be someone you trust to be inclusive of everyone's ideas, styles, and abilities, while also being comfortable making decisions on behalf of what's best for the team by thoughtfully balancing brand alignment, vision cohesion, and overall team strategy. The lead will loop in the broader team for additions, discussions, and new best practices or experiments.

This person can be a senior leader who wants to ensure certain best practices are consistently managed, or it can be someone with around two years on the team who has a good foundation balanced with great instincts. Someone who is relatively new to the team can participate in conjunction with either of the previously mentioned because new team members bring a great balance of new perspective and curiosity.

Process

Define the high-value moments that make your team's work effective. This is the overall methodology, the checklist of tasks, and the systems already in place that ensure your customers receive value. Think about it this way: When you onboard someone to a new project, what can you show them to get them up to speed as quickly as possible?

A few areas to consider:

- **Logistics:** any detailed information you need easy access to like common hotels to expensing processes
- **Templates:** anything from a presentation template to a well-written, frequently sent e-mail or calendar hold
- **Checklist:** an easily accessible list, or several lists, giving a quick snapshot of the required tasks

> **Reflect:** When you first joined your team, what were the structures or conversations that helped you understand the work your team did?

Technology

Define the tools that accelerate your people and enable your process. Find the right platform to visually display this ever-evolving blueprint. To do this, assess your team's current tools and, ideally, leverage an existing one that is easily accessible by the whole team. Ensure it can be quickly referenced and easily updated. This will be a living document, board, or spreadsheet, so whatever you use, make sure it can be easily referenced and edited. Most importantly, ensure the tool is secure. This is your team's intellectual property and should be treated as such.

Deploy Your Blueprint for Increased Engagement

When I was tasked with creating our team's first value blueprint, I felt responsible for producing a perfect list of team-wide best practices. I spent weeks trying to document multiple years worth of successful projects or evolving experiments.

In one-off conversations with teammates, I'd casually ask about their current project and the critical factors that led to the successful outcomes. Those conversations were helpful, but it still didn't feel like I was getting a detailed picture of what our value blueprint needed to involve.

I needed more of my team's input, beyond my one-off conversations. Looping in my team for broader perspectives was essential to the ultimate success of our blueprint as a source of valuable insights and practices. And not just because I was able to crowdsource the best practices but, more importantly, because I was able to bring the whole team along the process with me. This made the change management and overall usefulness of the blueprint as a tool long-lasting. Each of the five steps outlined below was enhanced by my team's input and involvement.

Once you have the people, processes, and technology for your blueprint, it's time to populate it with best practices, templates, and content. Start by mapping how you get work done today and then, with that foundation, improve the processes and dynamics with every cycle of effort.

Follow this process to build the foundation of your blueprint:

1. List all projects or work from the last 6 to 12 months or select 2 to 4 projects that fully represent the value your team delivers to customers.
2. Document everything about these projects to help you understand how your methods, work, and impact weave together. Reflect on the following:
   • What was the outcome the client/customer requested?

- What was the actual output delivered to the client/customer?
- What were the phases of work that led to these outputs and outcomes for our customers?
- What were the tangible and intangible elements that drove that outcome?
- What was the most meaningful or essential part of your process that made the outcome a success?
- What challenges occurred that hindered a high-quality outcome?
- What content, templates, lists, and documents can be tracked and repurposed for future projects?

3. Reflect on the content generated across the different projects in step 2 above. Identify, highlight, and theme the following:
   - What's different?
   - The same?
   - New?
   - Unique?

4. Extract the patterns from the content generated in the steps above and categorize them into themes. By diving into your client or customer's desired outcomes, you can better empathize with their needs. You might even find patterns across projects that highlight trends in core customer needs.

5. Define the best practices. Armed with the insights from steps 3 and 4, identify the following:
   - What are our customers asking of us? What are their core and consistent needs?
   - What are the common phases or customer interaction points reflected in each project experience listed?
   - What do we need to know so we don't make the same mistakes of the past?
   - What do we need to know so we can gain quick knowledge of the best path forward given specific variables?

Once you identify your baseline best practices, integrate them into the applicable phase of your blueprint for easy future reference. The phases can be as simple as three to five steps or you can bring in more nuance and specificity by going up to eight steps. The priority is to ensure every team member knows where to look for information they need.

Phases can be as simple as:

1. Intake
2. Engage
3. Execute
4. Retrospective

Or even simpler:

1. Pre-Work
2. Work
3. Post-Work

Leverage your team throughout this process. Crowdsourcing information is a great way to lay the initial foundation of your blueprint's best practices, as well as capitalize on the creative thought and diverse expertise across your team.

> **Insight:** Identifying best practices accelerates both new and existing teammates by giving access to proven practices that reduce repeat mistakes and address challenges before they occur.

Experiment Big and Small to Grow

We're constantly experimenting on our team. Sometimes the outcome sticks for a long time and sometimes it's relevant and engaging for a specific period. Most Fridays on our team were *Frydays*, where we'd source French fries from different restaurants near our office and whoever was available would gather in a conference room to eat lunch and share our opinions on whether Tater Tots counted as a French fry. This started because two people on the team happened to buy fries from two different places on the same Friday. And, after that, everyone was engaged by either purchasing more fry options or indulging in the purchases and providing their opinion on the "best" fry in town. This experiment and ritual didn't last forever but, for a few months, it was engaging, brought the team together, and didn't take a huge amount of team-wide effort to implement.

A more customer-facing example was when we experimented with hosting a collaborative, hands-on meeting with some attendees on the phone and others in person. We experimented with a liaison role that would create a bridge between the workshop participant on the phone and the in-person attendees. We experimented with this method a handful of times and ultimately determined that the effort outweighed the benefit. Additionally, we found the complexity of the dual setup took away from everyone's overall experience and ability to add value.

The blueprint is an ongoing, full team effort. Once you have the baseline structure established by leveraging the steps described in the previous sections, you want to make sure the blueprint stays alive and does not stagnate. Experimentation and continued discussions are at the core of this phase of value blueprinting.

Determine Cadence

It is essential to determine the timing and cadence at the beginning of this process. Otherwise, the reinforcement of best practices won't occur as easily or as quickly. Remember, integrating value blueprinting, like any new team-wide process, requires thoughtful change management. Craft specific, recurring times to review and update the blueprint both individually and as a team.

The cadence will change at different stages of the process. Initially, you might want to review it more frequently, weekly, or every two weeks. Eventually, for most teams, settling into a monthly cadence is sufficient for refreshers and ongoing maintenance.

Leverage Retrospectives

Monthly reviews are great for maintenance check-ins. In addition to monthly reviews, weave retrospectives into your post project process—a great best practice for your blueprint, if it's not already in there. Learnings from a recently completed project or a significant project milestone keep your blueprint alive and relevant. Retrospectives help everyone reflect on immediate learnings from a recent client engagement or product experience. Design the retrospectives in a way to easily inform your blueprint.

Drive Experiments

Deep process discussions across the team often result in curiosities. Rather than debating whether something should be in the blueprint as a best practice, run an experiment.

Experiments are critical for your team because they ensure you remain competitive and relevant. Experiments for blueprinting can be tricky, however, because you need to determine the number of times something needs to be tested to be validated. You also need to understand what you are trying to achieve or learn with the experiment. Is it a specific part of the process you want to improve with this experiment? Or is this a new idea or innovation for which you're trying to find an application? Understanding the why behind the experiment will make the experimentation and reflection process easier as you progress.

There are two critical processes to support your experiments:

1. Appoint a lead who reminds the team to apply the experiment. The lead also looks out for relevant opportunities for the experiment and taps people to drive it forward. In short, the lead ensures follow-up and follow-through.
2. Review experiment results and optimize. Review experiment results to make decisions on how to leverage learnings to optimize your blueprint. As part of the review process, you will decide if:
   - This should be a permanent part of the blueprint.
   - This will be a recommended best practice within certain conditions, and outline those conditions.
   - This was a one-off and shouldn't be integrated into the blueprint.

Insight: The blueprinting process is an ongoing, full-team effort.

Reflect, Evolve, Repeat

The Fusion team delivers ideas, methods, and techniques that create high-performing teams, and we can do that because of continuous iterations to our blueprint.

With many processes, there's a step that encourages repeating the steps again. In this case, the steps are those we previously defined to build the foundation of your blueprint. The secret is knowing when to evolve and repeat that process. That's where team-wide reflection and experimentation are essential.

In 2020, our team had to quickly shift our in-person model to a virtual one due to the COVID-19 pandemic. Unlike my story at the start of this chapter, my team did not have any solidified best practices around a virtual model for our offerings. Our approach to evolving our work relied heavily on learning from existing models and our own rapid experimentation.

Looking back, we could have documented some of our best practices earlier on when we did virtual sessions. However, because these were rare occurrences and covered a small percentage of our vast scope of work, we didn't give those instances much attention as part of our core blueprint.

Despite this massive industry shift, success remained at the intersection between our customer's core needs and our team's value-based offering. We just needed to spend some time identifying the value at those intersections.

The key was taking the time to identify the values that we wanted to amplify in this new, virtual model. Some values remained the same as our in-person model, such as focusing on the people we serve. New values emerged because of the new virtual dynamic. You achieve a successful outcome when you identify your customers' core needs even as they change, and continually evolve your own offering to satisfy their needs.

Going through the value blueprint process through this new lens helped our team solidify our values and identify the right tools and processes to support our customer's evolving needs. Capitalizing on this moment, we rebuilt our team's blueprint to remain relevant, competitive, and, most importantly, effective.

Key Takeaways

Own Your Process

Map everything you do, review it, experiment with it, and iterate on it. The process of blueprinting your work allows you to own your process and remain on the cutting edge. Your first step is to analyze your team's last 2-4 projects and extract themes of the learnings, successes, and outcomes.

Conduct Regular Maintenance

By going through this process every few years, or when a major market shift occurs, you will more deeply understand your core purpose and further elevate what makes your offering unique. Stay in tune with what your customers value and how those needs evolve over time. Do this by talking to your customers directly, reviewing outcomes, and asking them about the value your team provided.

Leverage Your Team

Your team has a breadth of knowledge, expertise, and insight. Leverage your people to elevate your blueprint through added detail and variety. As a first step, establish retrospectives for different project milestones and solicit best practices from that recent work.

CHAPTER 9

Elite Team Structure

By Caitlin Geissler

Picture a team, any team. It could be your current team; a team you've been on in the past; it could be a favorite sports team, a gaming team, or a debate team. Picture that team and think about its primary attributes. As you are visualizing this team, you might be thinking of the people on the team, what those individuals were aiming to achieve, how well that team performed to those objectives, and, perhaps, you're thinking about what did not work quite so well on the team. If, at this moment, we were able to survey every reader and collect their thoughts, we would likely see strong clustering around these particular themes. While the word "team" will conjure different associations for different people, once we say team, we often gravitate toward the same attributes of people, objectives, and performance. The decision that precedes this is what we find to be the singular most important decision: the intentional choice to be a team.

In our years of working within a Fortune 10 enterprise, we've worked with groups of people, and we've worked with teams. Our approach to each is different because there is an inherent difference between a group of individuals and a team. This insight only became clear when we observed the variations in outcomes, collaboration, mindset, and resilience. Teams arrived at better outcomes than groups, and exceptional teams produced extraordinary results as compared to both "teams" and "groups." Decoding this insight led us to a fundamental theory: choosing to be a team in identity, structure, and achievement creates a magnification of positive impact and opportunity.

Several principles support our fundamental theory of team structure and consistently generate positive impact and continued opportunity (Figure 9.1).

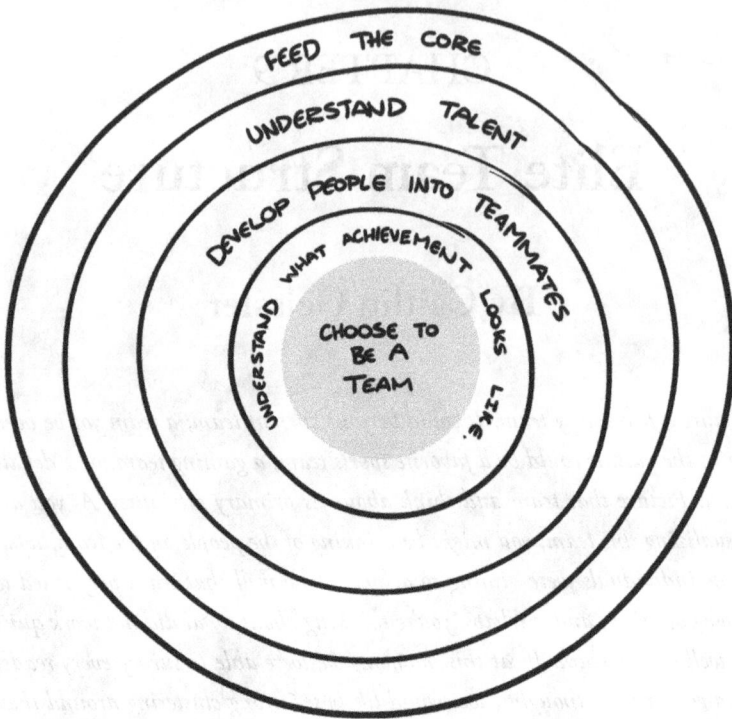

Figure 9.1 Fundamental team principles

By implementing a solid team structure and focusing on these principles, anything becomes possible.

Principle 1: Choose to Be a Team

A team can be a group, but a group isn't always a team. Choose to be a team. In the early days of forming our team, we made a choice not to follow a hierarchy of roles and be an organization, but to follow the hierarchy of a team and be teammates. The team was the most important priority, then our teammates, and then ourselves. With four or so people on the team, it was easy to keep an eye on all three levels: Team is good, teammates are good, and I'm good—check!

As a team, however small we were, we defined the fundamental elements that made us a team:

- A team name and articulated identity
- A structure for how we worked
- A shared and understood objective
- Principles for how we showed up for each other
- A collective mindset

Identity, Structure, and Objective

As we grew, we added teammates who were diverse from the initial few. We had skillsets we didn't have before, and we had the ability to do work we weren't able to do before. Our identity needed to be defined so that we could effectively welcome our new teammates into the team and to what we were doing. We are Fusion, we are an enterprise accelerator, and we are here to help. Our identity was clear and strong enough that as we added these teammates our identity was magnified rather than augmented. New teammates immediately shared in this identity, were able to work within it, and succeeded as a result of it.

The focus placed on building and bestowing ownership of the team identity to all of us was like wearing an invisible jersey. As a point of pride and expectation, we had to represent and convey the identity of our team in everything we did, no matter where we were. When we work with teams—whether newly forming or those looking to elevate—we focus on identity. It may require hours to hone the answer to, "Who are you?" but the unified response of, "We are . . . , and we believe . . ." is a powerful moment for a team.

A team's structure stems from identity and is the active thread that connects identity and objective (Figure 9.2). Structure forms when teammates choose to work with (and for) each other as they seek to achieve the team's objective. If you're forming a basketball team, the objective might be winning the league championship. The team structure will then be guided by how the team pursues the objective: Practice twice a day, stay in peak physical shape, work on fundamentals, understand plays, value the assist as much as taking the three-pointer, and know your competition better than they understand you. Whatever the objective of your team, it needs to be clear and understood so that the structure can be effective. Consistently elevating and acting according to the key elements of your defined principles and mindset will help you create structure.

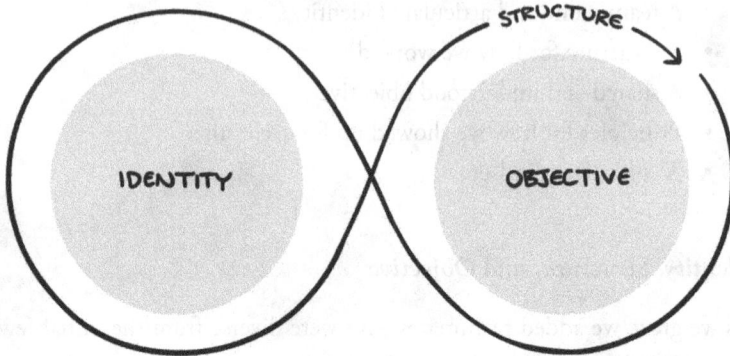

Figure 9.2 Team structure loop

Principles

Principles guide behaviors and set norms. Just as we've defined principles to support and actualize the theories in this book, you can create principles to support and actualize the identity and structure of your team. The principles you set with your team become a binding construct between teammates. They create a fascinating unspoken language between teammates, which enables one another to anticipate actions and respond to each other without speaking.

Our team has 13 principles we adhere to. They are visible in our physical team space, as well as digitally, to be wherever we are. These principles are among the first things that new teammates learn. As an example, one of our principles is: Always Take Notes. This might seem like a trivial principle. However, for the work we do and for how often we're doing research interviews, this one principle builds a database of insight. It builds a trust that teammates have our backs if a technical glitch arises or if we're focused on leading the conversation. The Hierarchy of Priorities for a high-performing team (Figure 9.3) begins by thinking about the team first, then your teammates, and then yourself. Team principles flow through a similar hierarchy which will dive deeper into the sections ahead.

As your team creates your principles, consider the critical elements of your identity, your structure, and your objective. Craft principles to ensure behaviors are created, which inherently and consistently result in the outcomes you're seeking to produce. Your team should build your

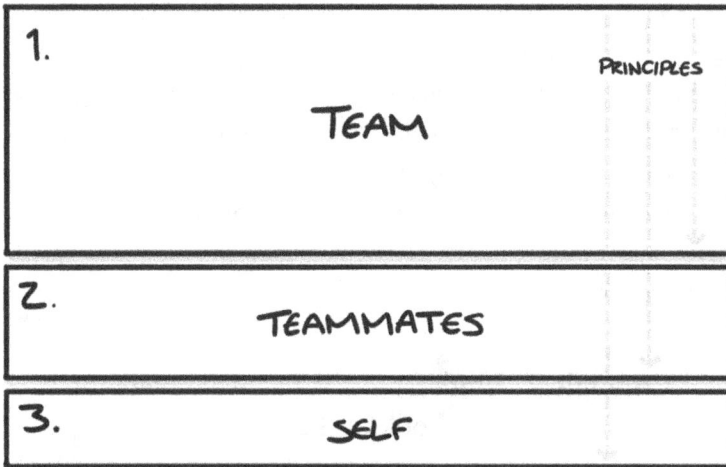

Figure 9.3 Team hierarchy of priorities

principles together. This is an essential exercise in building collaboration, shared ownership of the team identity, and a sense of alignment toward your team's objective. By initiating this exercise, you create a space for sharing and begin to condition comfort in open conversations around what matters most.

Mindset

In previous chapters, you've read about the importance of diversity of thought, ideas, perspectives, and experiences. This is indeed exceedingly important when you're aiming to form an elite-level team. Having a collective mindset, then, might seem counter to this guidance. The collective mindset a team shares is, as with other aspects, an intentional choice of what the team finds acceptable for its identity. There is an intentional shared mindset of performance, presentation, achievement, challenges, and obstacles that an elite team will share.

Our team's mindset explores the positive, the possible, and the exploratory. We function in that collective mindset in the work we do, individually and together. As individuals, we each have diverse mindsets and lived experiences that we apply to our work (e.g., global humanitarian mindset) yet, collectively, we share the chosen and aspiring *team* mindset (e.g., positive, possible, and exploratory mindset).

In your team's collaboration on defining principles, you'll begin to see from which collective mindset your team wishes to function. If you're a fundraising team, you might gravitate toward fundraising principles that form long partnerships instead of one-time small donations. A shared mindset might then center on deeply valuing the time and personal connections of donors.

Principle 2: Understand What Achievement Looks Like

The choice of being a team demands an emphasis on performance—both individually and collectively. As a team, it is essential to understand what winning looks like and to be supported in achieving that expectation. Performance matters on a team. After setting team objectives, a team begins to aspire to a level of performance that helps them reach those goals. Participation isn't enough; likewise, being on the team isn't enough. The team and the individuals on the team must both perform.

A few years into the development of our team, we grew by adding several exceptional individuals. In an early conversation with these new teammates, we set the expectation on performance by stating that, as team members, you get to assume ownership and connection to all past successes and future successes of the team. All Fusion team members get to say "we did this" because you are value-contributing members of this team. "Value contributing" is the key element in the previous sentence. Everyone on the team, new or old, has the ability to perform and contribute value. The legacy of the team gets to be shared by those who add to its legacy. The achievement of the individual increases the chances of achievement by the team.

Individual Achievement

Achievement is often associated with substantial or significant moments. Yet, the principle of understanding achievement focuses across all moments—big and small, significant or seemingly less than. The reason we emphasize this across all moments is because they all matter. If we only waited for, focused on, or celebrated big wins, we'd miss the opportunity to highlight individual growth, personal breakthroughs, and the overcoming of challenges which may not be monumental to team results but are monumental to the individuals' progress.

Focusing on achievement in all moments also increases opportunities for coaching, assessment, and feedback. Again, consider the example of a basketball team. If the athletes were only coached or given feedback during games, then the hours of practice would be a missed opportunity for individuals to advance their skills to expected performance. We view this similarly in an enterprise setting. There will be the game-time moments—presentations, project deliverables, product launches—yet, it is the moments in between where the greatest opportunities for individual achievement and performance may occur. For individuals on the team, knowing that all moments are performance moments can bring a positive level of intensity to that work.

An important note here is that we're not specifically emphasizing results. In fact, we've somewhat decoupled performance from results. The reason why we draw attention to the distinction is that sometimes, an individual might perform incredibly well but the results aren't achieved, and other times, an individual might perform poorly, and the result is achieved. For example, on a sports team, a player might have played terribly by not executing the plays to the expectation of the position, but still, they won the game. Focusing only on the result doesn't progress the individual player's ability. Conversely, a player might play exceptionally well, executing every play to expectation, but ultimately lose the game. Results are important and we want to work toward a strong correlation between exceptional performance and exceptional results, but we should not discount the moments when the two don't align. Individual achievement should focus on the individual.

Team Achievement

Understanding what team achievement looks like shares aspects of individual performance, but it isn't a pure equation of *individual* + *individual* = *team achievement*. Drawing back to our choice to be a team, there is an emphasis on achieving *together*. We will again look at achievement across all moments big and small. Yet, when working as a team, we will be more focused on results. Team achievement is about lifting each other up to get to the expected level of performance and results.

In team achievement scenarios, be clear on the objective and what "winning" looks like. Analysis of the work to be done and the expectation of achievement should inform which individuals you select for that work. Critical considerations should be placed on how you might be able to achieve the intended results while maximizing the development of your team. You'll read more about creating opportunities for individuals and ensuring success in Chapter 10, "Team System."

Principle 3: Build People into Teammates

In the team hierarchy of priorities (Figure 9.4), we outlined thinking about the team first, then your teammates, and then yourself. If we were to draw a direct line from team to self, we would overlook the heartbeat of a team. In speaking with different teams, leaders, and individuals who are looking to increase their team performance and culture, we will some-times hear repetition of a phrase like, "I try to do my best for the team." This is a really encouraging statement because it does show the emphasis

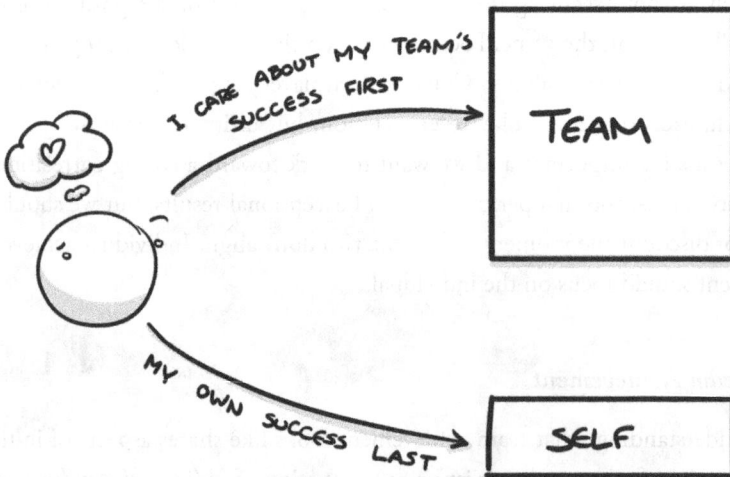

Figure 9.4 Hierarchy of priorities without teammate focus

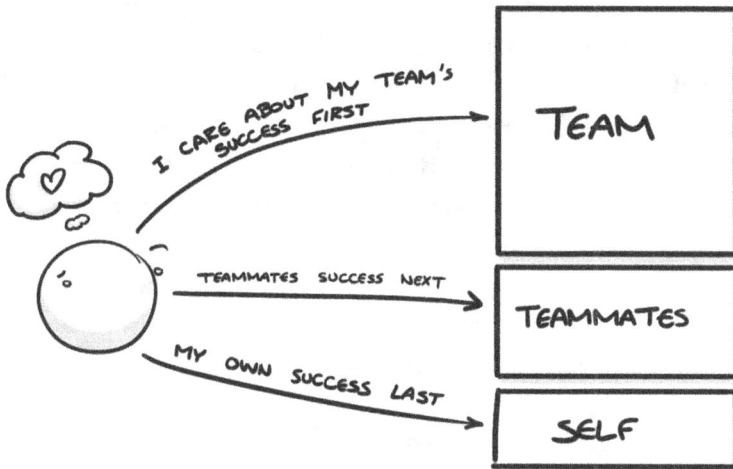

Figure 9.5 Hierarchy of priorities with teammate focus

of team-first. What we find, however, is that the missing link is the development of individuals into *teammates* (Figure 9.5). Many of us will have experienced this in our careers. We're welcomed onto a team and trained on what our role is and what success looks like, yet we're not trained on how we can make each other successful.

Exceptional teams take the time to do this training and emphasize this mode of operating as a valuable priority. When we make this one mental shift to think about team, teammates, and then self, we begin to hear phrases, such as, "How can I support you?" or "I can help you with that."

Better still, when we make this shift, we observe teammates acting in the success of each other. No need to ask or offer, teammates create a flow state of anticipating and enabling success for each other. Learning how to be an incredible teammate and building a team of incredible teammates is a lasting skill for leaders at all levels.

Principle 4: Identify Talent

Identifying talent is a continuous process on a team and is owned by everyone, not just leaders and managers. As a specific principle supporting the theory of team structure, when we say, "identifying talent," we are referring to identifying the talent which resides within your team, as well as the talent you need on your team, which could be developed within a teammate. We approach this as profiling for positivity.

Profiling for positivity is the exercise of understanding the finest attributes, skills, and abilities of each teammate. This is an undertaking shared by everyone on the team and is a critical component of being an exceptional teammate. As teammates working together, working in support of each other's success, and working toward the success of the team, astutely observing the talents displayed by teammates—talents they may not be aware of—is essential. Success in the principle is realized when a teammate is able to state the best qualities of any teammate without preparation or warning.

The next level to this exercise is observing what essential talents the team lacks, which may possibly be developed within a teammate. Design moments for talent growth and create the time and space for success.

Principle 5: Feed the Core

The core of a team is owned by all team members. The core is defined by the team; it includes identity, structure, culture, strategy, production, and expertise. Each dimension defined as core by a team must be understood and fed. You've already seen some detailed examples of systems that feed the core in Chapter 6, "Artists and Scientists" and Chapter 8, "Value Blueprinting."

The development of a system that perpetually feeds the core dimensions of a team takes some initial planning. However, the task becomes much easier once the behavior pattern becomes a memory. If we use strategy as an example (Figure 9.6), a repeatable pattern can be found in the following:

- **Explore:** Be intentional with exploration into a strategy model relevant to your objectives.
- **Experiment:** Design experiments that let you test the new models you discover.
- **Return value to the core:** Evaluate your findings, identify the value, and return that value to the core.

The core then becomes a place from which the rest of the team can draw knowledge, experience, and inspiration.

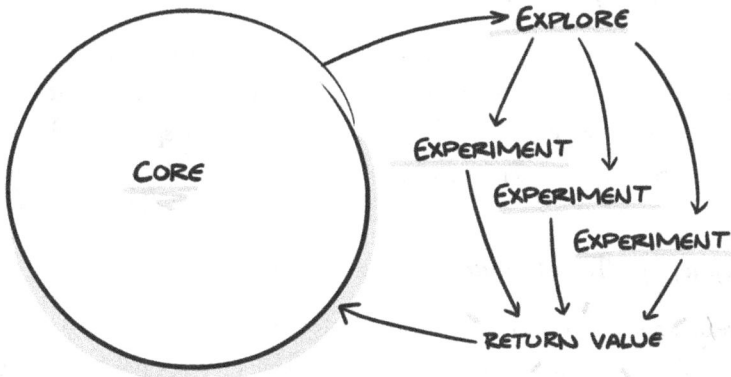

Figure 9.6 Feed the core

This pattern creates a deeper ability to thread insights and connect dots which, in turn, gives the team an advantage when pursuing its objectives. As a team, you more deeply know your community, your market, your industry, and your competition. The key to success in this principle is making this work primary to the team's structure. We often hear of teams doing this type of work on an annual or quarterly basis. Yet, just as we don't want to wait for only the significant moments to measure achievement, we don't want to miss critical moments for expanding opportunity and impact from the continuous exploration and evolution of the team's core.

> **Reflect:** How has your team made—or how can your team make—the specific and conscious choice to be a team? What future might that enable for you?

Key Takeaways

Take action. The five principles outlined in this chapter detail proven methods and mindset shifts that support the intentional formation of a team and lead to a magnification of impact and opportunity. As you go forward in your own team's growth and development, we encourage you to think of where you are, what your destination is, and then take action incrementally with your team. The key to any great journey of growth is starting. To help you on that path, here are some key first steps:

Create Space for a Team Identity Conversation

Gather your team together virtually or in person. Then, create a fill-in-the-blanks style collaboration by having the team respond to "We are . . . , we believe . . . , we create . . ."—there is no limit to the responses and there are no wrong answers. From the ideation, create a team identity statement.

Define, as a Team, What Achievement Looks Like

Create an environment where individuals can share where they want to grow. Focus on team achievements by asking what can be done together.

Emphasize Teammate Success

Create a team ritual around acting in the success of teammates.

Identify Talent

Set an expectation of the team to scan for the positive attributes and abilities of their teammates.

Take a first step in, as a team, defining the core dimensions of your team. Once defined, take one, simple action to ensure the core is sustained.

CHAPTER 10

Team System

By Trey Bliss

Every person on an elite team is a leader in their own unique way—whether a leader in their role, an initiative, or a unique perspective they bring to the team. In this chapter, "leader" refers to people who embody the spirit of a leader, not simply those with authority.

The renowned football coach Vince Lombardi once said, "Individual commitment to a group effort—that is what makes a team work, a company work, a society work, a civilization work."[1] This quote is often lauded for its focus on group effort. Yet, it's the "individual commitment" we want to explore here. Individual commitment to what? Individual commitment to your work is important, no doubt, but it's the individual commitment to one another that separates *elite* teams from ordinary teams (Figure 10.1).

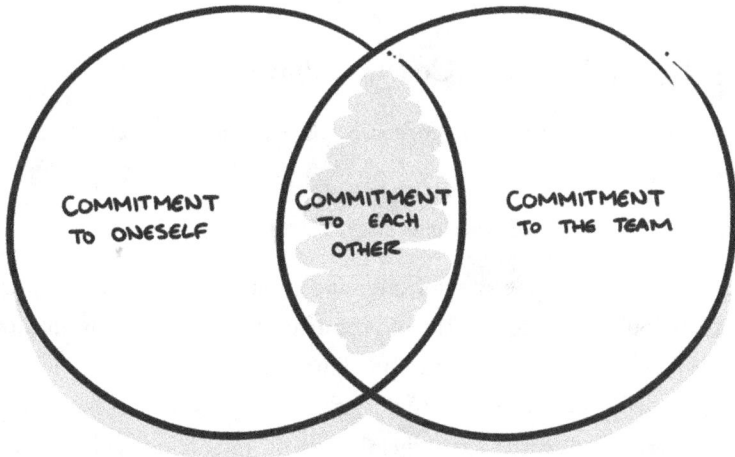

Figure 10.1 Commitment Venn diagram

After all, a team at its core is simply a group of individuals who have many interactions every day. These interactions span large projects and small tasks. Whether it is formally defined or a set of unwritten rules, each team has a system for how these interactions occur. Every team has ways they ask for support, ask questions, or collaborate on important decisions. Like a computer's operating system, which enables programs to communicate with hardware, a Team Operating System controls how different parts of your team communicate and interact. A well-implemented Team Operating System can drive high performance at any level of a company.

A Team Operating System is something that is often overlooked when teams are forming, but it is crucial to a team's success. When discussing team interaction and communication, it can be helpful to use a sports team as a lens. The manager is like the coach, team leaders are team captains and team members are players. The Team Operating System defines and supports how these roles interact.

A Team Operating System applies to the way you view your team members and the perspectives your entire team shares as they work together. There are three key areas you need to target to correctly implement a Team Operating System that maximizes your team's talent:

1. Do your job.
2. Create opportunities for growth.
3. Enable success and take responsibility for failure.

Do Your Job: Coaches, Players, Leaders

What does it mean to be an elite coach, player, or team leader?

Coach—An Essential Role of a High-Performing Team

Coaches serve as a guide, mentor, and tone-setter for their team. In sports, coaches don't just delegate tasks and commands. They are responsible for the growth of their players both individually and collectively. They give motivational pregame speeches and reflective postgame speeches. They build relationships with each of their players on and off the field. Coaches set the bar and it's up to their team to meet it.

A team in a corporate setting feeds off their manager's energy. If the manager approaches a project with a "let's-just-get-by" attitude, then you can be sure that the team will respond with barely acceptable work. If a manager presents a new project with excitement and views it as an opportunity for the team, the energy surrounding that project will drive much better results.

Furthermore, coaches and managers cultivate team members' talent. Talent alone is not enough. You've probably heard this statement countless times throughout your life and for good reason. Just possessing talent is never enough. How that talent is used, groomed, and deployed can differentiate between a team that drives massive impact and a team that simply does their job. Another way to say this is: coaching matters.

Take the case of the Golden State Warriors, an NBA dynasty that won three championships between 2015 and 2018. In 2013 and 2014, Mark Jackson was their coach, and they were a competent team, amassing a record of 51-31. The team already had a collection of elite players with unique skill sets. Stephen Curry and Klay Thompson formed the best shooting backcourt in basketball history and were surrounded by a cast of mid-sized, cerebral forwards. Additionally, they had elite individual defenders in Draymond Green and Andre Iguodala. But something was missing. In late 2014 Mark Jackson was fired, and Steve Kerr was brought on as head coach. He changed the way the team played, restructuring the offense around his players' skills. The system was dubbed "small ball" for its frenzied pace and ideal blend of court spacing, ball movement, and three-point shooting. The 2015 team achieved a record of 65-17 and won the NBA championship.[2] The roster makeup was largely the same and the competitive landscape in the league didn't shift, so what changed? Coaching matters. Mark Jackson was a great basketball coach, but Steve Kerr built a team system that maximized his roster's talent. He had great shooters, so he built a system around shooting. His best players were smaller in stature, so he tailored his system for speed rather than size.

An enterprise differs from basketball in many ways, but there are lessons we can take from Steve Kerr's Warriors about coaching. Coaches set their team up to be as successful as they can be. They funnel work to the team and make large decisions about the work their team pursues. We will do a deep dive into elite coaching later in the book but what's important is: elite coaching will elevate your team to heights that were previously considered impossible.

Team Leader—The Inspiration

Another critical role in any successful team is team leader. The team leader is much closer to the team member role and often occupies both roles simultaneously. In sports, this position is called a team captain, and at the office, these leaders may not be formally recognized as such, but they are just as impactful as the coach or manager. In some ways, team leaders are an extension of the coach, who can't be everywhere at once.

There is one unique thing about the role of team leader: on an elite team, anyone can be a team leader at any time. This could mean taking the lead on a project, being an advocate for a team-wide initiative, or becoming a subject matter expert. Elite teams encourage each other to step up and be a leader in various ventures. On our team, the same person could occupy a supporting role on one project and lead another. This fluidity enhances our team's efficacy and drives value in any situation because anyone with experience or a value-add feels comfortable as the primary driver for a project.

Additionally, allowing people to step in and out of the team leader role helps team members feel more empowered. A meta-analysis of 105 studies on empowering leaders found that empowered employees translate to more confident individuals who have faith their ideas have value. This confidence becomes visible during team discussions where individuals share their ideas without fear of a negative reaction. Providing individuals with autonomy causes employees to feel more invested in their work, which deepens their belief that they can make a difference.[3]

These are all effects of a properly implemented team leader role. Maybe your team already has designated team leaders, but that shouldn't stop you from stepping up to be a team leader whenever possible.

Player—The Lifeblood of the Team

Players refer to people who implement strategies, use technologies, and complete tasks that are delegated by the coaches and team leaders. Team leaders are also players and, in an enterprise, setting Coaches may also occupy the player role. While it is a coach's responsibility to architect and communicate the Team Operating System, it's the players who put that system to work.

Players can be developers, business analysts, systems analysts, designers, architects, administrative personnel, and everything in between. Therefore, it is critical that the players buy into the System. If each individual is fully engaged and attentive to how they should support one another and communicate, it doesn't matter what specific role they occupy. Correctly implementing a Team Operating System, allows team members to maximize their potential while taking every opportunity to support others.

Attitude and energy begin with the coach but, in many ways, communication begins with the players. Players need to communicate with their coach and team leaders about their capacity to avoid becoming overwhelmed. They must also communicate with their team to build relationships and ensure successful collaboration. It's a lot of responsibility to be a player on an elite team, but a great Team Operating System and supportive leadership can set you up for success.

"Do your job" is a commonly heard phrase in the world of team sports. By understanding the purpose behind your role and fulfilling your role to its fullest, you can ensure that your team is as successful as possible.

> **Reflection:** Who are the coaches, team leaders, and players on your team? How can these roles be better defined?

Create Opportunities for Growth

One of the best ways to grow a Team Operating System is to grow the people within it. We have touched on individual growth in other chapters, and our focus here is team growth. Growing together in an enterprise environment can be challenging because individuals are working to shine. An elite team knows that the best way to promote yourself is to promote your team by actively seeking opportunities for growth. There are three main pillars of opportunity creation that allow elite teams to consistently accomplish this goal:

1. Fluidity of roles
2. Understanding the situation
3. Recognizing the value of early wins

Fluidity of Roles: Cover and Move

We previously discussed how the role of a team leader is fluid and provides a wide range of benefits to their team. This fluidity should be extended to all roles within the team. It's important to note that "roles" in this case are not referring to the three specified roles (coach, team leader, player) although those roles may also fluctuate. In this case, "roles" refers to a role within a specific environment or task. For example, you might take the lead at one interview and then be a notetaker at another. Or you may be responsible for the design of one slide presentation while you help provide the content for another. This fluidity allows each person to pursue many growth areas. It also allows the team to effectively employing the "Cover and Move" strategy in times of low capacity or emergency. Cover and Move refers to a team's ability to call on each other for help or even make a full substitution on a project or task if something arises. Complications will inevitably arise in a fast-paced corporate environment so the ability to provide last-minute support is crucial.

There are limitations to how fluid your team can be. Technical skills and other areas of expertise may not allow a team to fully occupy every role at any time, but familiarity and experience in a variety of situations can drastically improve your team's ability to communicate. You may never be a user experience (UX) expert, but occasionally immersing yourself in a UX role will give you tools to communicate with your UX counterparts.

You might wonder how risky it is to let someone complete a task they lack skills for, or work in an unfamiliar area. This is where the concept of a low-risk task comes into play. Every team in an enterprise setting has a spectrum of tasks that can be evaluated across two dimensions: *priority* and *risk*, as shown in Figure 10.2. High-priority/low-risk tasks are prime opportunities for teammates to stretch their comfort levels, learn new skills, and grow. They can also provide early wins that bolster confidence in new skills and encourage development. You can be an ally and advocate for team growth by actively identifying high-priority/low-risk opportunities for fellow teammates.

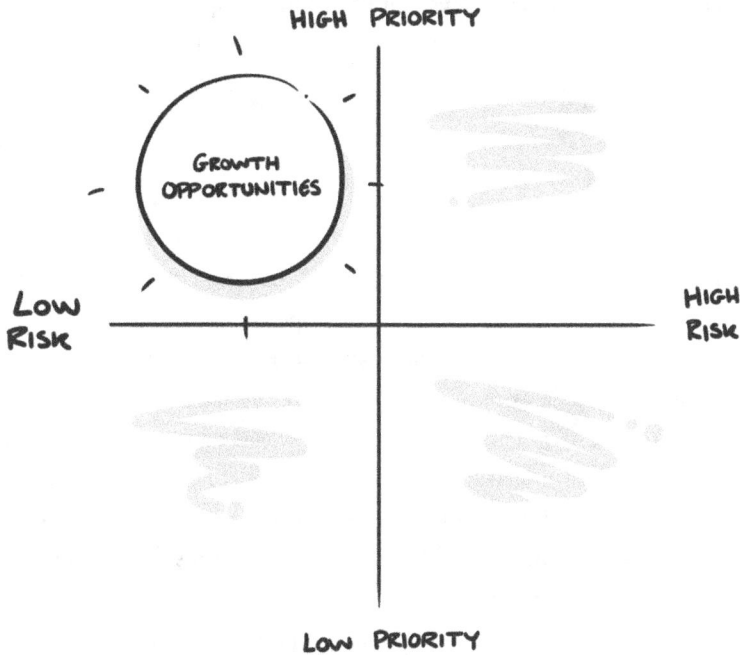

Figure 10.2 Opportunity assessment

Understand the Situation: Protect Your Teammates

Understanding the situation is key to support your team members' growth, and continually build trust among your team. As a member of an elite team, you should always be looking to set your teammates up for success, even while you pursue your own opportunities to shine. Larry Bird is widely considered one of the greatest basketball players to ever set foot on the court. He was a stalwart on the Boston Celtics during the 1980s and early 1990s. But what's most impressive about him is that he constantly sought opportunities to make his teammates better even as he built on his own successes. Over his career, Bird racked up 5,695 assists good for 3rd in all-time Celtics franchise history.[4] He knew that providing his teammates with great opportunities gave his team the best chance to win. When it got down to crunch time, everyone knew who was taking the last shot. Although Larry Bird was a willing passer, at the end of games he understood that his shot gave them the best chance to win. Operating within an elite team is no different. Always be on the lookout for ways to assist your teammates, whether that's providing support, offering growth opportunities, or sharing the credit. As a leader, you must also understand the situation and know when to take the shot yourself.

Value Early Wins: Generate Momentum

The last pillar of opportunity creation within your Team Operating System is recognizing the value of early wins. Like recognizing a low-risk situation, leaders must also recognize the opportunity to give a teammate, themselves, or the team as a whole a quick win. A quick win could be something as simple as sending a beautifully formatted e-mail to introduce your team to a client or inviting a new leader in your company to meet with your team about their vision and goals. Anything that showcases what differentiates you from other people or teams can be a quick win. The benefit here is two-fold: A quick win will instill confidence in your teammate and builds a winning culture.

In 2009, a team from Harvard Business Review conducted a survey of 5,400 new leaders and their managers to discover how their habits and practices correlated to their performance. What they found was that most of the high-performing leaders had managed to secure a quick win early on.[5] A quick win not only builds self-confidence in the individual who got the win, it also helps to assure others of their ability to succeed.

To build an elite team you must also craft a winning culture by consistently drilling your team on the right habits and behaviors that correlate to success. By valuing quick wins and recognizing when you can set a team member up for a win you can drive the creation of that culture.

Creating opportunities for one another is a staple of any elite team. It's a sign that your group is tight-knit and trusts each other to routinely deliver results. Additionally, actively seeking opportunities for one another is an excellent way for teams to develop a variety of skills.

> **Reflection:** Think of three areas in which members on your team could grow. Now try to identify a few tasks that would facilitate growth in those areas.

Enable Success and Take Responsibility for Failure

No one likes to fail. We hate coming up short in any game, test, or challenge. But failure is a part of life. As we've discussed, leaders find opportunities for their teammates and employees to be successful, but there is a flip side to this coin. Leaders also take responsibility for failure. This creates a sense of trust and comfort for those operating in their environment that allows others to flourish. By knowing when to intervene and take a "hit" for their team, leaders will earn the respect and loyalty of their employees and peers.

Intervene Accordingly

Knowing when to intervene is challenging. It requires an understanding of the situation and the people in it. Great Leaders put effort into knowing their team. This way they can gauge a situation and decide whether to intervene.

Imagine that you have identified an amazing business strategy opportunity. There is an ask from somewhere in your company to consult on a market analysis and you have encouraged someone on your team, let's call them Ashley, to volunteer for the project. Ashley doesn't have as much business strategy experience as others, and you feel she would rise to the challenge and benefit from the experience. At first, the project is going great. Soon you learn that the output will be presented to a cut-throat executive who is known for grilling presenters. You now have a decision to make: Do you trust Ashley to represent the team in this endeavor or do you intervene?

This is an important project that will reflect on the entire team, but intervening could shake Ashley's confidence and discourage her from pursuing new opportunities. To navigate the situation, you must communicate with Ashley as soon as the complication occurs. Reassure her that you know she's doing great work and be candid about your concerns. It's now your call whether to step in and help guide Ashley or make a substitution and tag someone else to lead the project. If you decide to substitute, you must make it clear to Ashley that it is your failure, not hers, for incorrectly reading the situation.

This example highlights the nuances great leaders must navigate. Knowing when to intervene can be tricky and there is no one-size-fits-all answer. As the leader of a team, project, or routine task, you will find yourself in similar situations. If you handle those situations with honesty, understanding, and decisiveness then you will be on your way to enabling your team.

Take the Hit for Your Team: Demonstrate Accountability

Great leaders take the hit for their team. Taking full responsibility for a team, project, or task is what leading is all about. If things go well, you will likely receive the lion's share of credit, even if you try to pass that credit along to your team. In turn, when things go poorly you should bear the brunt of the blame. This thought process is embodied by a concept called Extreme Ownership, developed by Jocko Willink. Willink explains that he once led a Navy SEAL team in the Iraq war. One day on patrol gunfire erupted on the battlefield. Enemy fire mixed with friendly fire and friendly forces. Americans and Iraqis were firing against each other. The incident left one friendly Iraqi soldier dead and numerous Iraqi and American soldiers wounded. Someone was going to be held responsible. The question of who was at fault swirled around. Was it the Iraqi forces? Was it an American soldier? Was it one of Jocko's Navy SEALs? When the commanding officer gathered all the SEALs together to investigate the situation, there was only one answer he received. "I was the senior officer on the battlefield. It was my fault." Jocko told the room.[6] That's Extreme Ownership in practice.

Our team lives by this concept every day. On our team, if you are the lead of a year-long engagement or a task that takes a day to complete then you own it. This displays to your team, senior leaders, and clients that you can handle the responsibility of any undertaking. It shows the individuals supporting you or working for you that you are never going to push blame onto them. This attitude trickles down into the most routine of tasks until everyone takes full ownership of everything they do. That's why taking the hit for your team is so important. It causes a ripple effect that motivates everyone on the team to strive for success.

Knowing when to intervene and how to take responsibility are intangible traits that vastly increase leadership ability and support any elite team. As a leader, you may not always make the right decision or deploy the right personnel for a project. But being transparent and owning your decisions can ensure that whatever the outcome, you will maintain your team's respect and loyalty.

> **Reflection:** Think of the last time you failed at a task or project, did you bear the brunt of responsibility or blame circumstance? How could you have owned that failure more completely?

Teamwork is a difficult subject to define because teamwork is about what exists among multiple individuals. It is an interplay that is concurrently unmeasurable and yet so observable that an outsider can tell within minutes how well a team works together. One thing is certain, when properly employed, elite teamwork can propel even the most mundane individuals to outstanding results.

Elite teamwork is challenging, and properly implementing and maintaining a Team Operating System enables individuals to reach their potential without hindering the rest of the group. It is crucial that every person on your team buys-in to the Team Operating System and understands their responsibility to uphold, as well as grow, the team.

Elite Teams are groups of uniquely skilled individuals who, together, develop each other, grow each other, and, most importantly, lead each other. To be considered elite, each person on your team must do their job, create opportunities for growth, and enable success but as well as take responsibility for failure. After all, as Helen Keller once said, "Alone we can do so little; together we can do so much."[7]

Key Takeaways

Below are three key steps to begin defining your team system:

Define Your Roles

Clearly defined roles and expectations allow team members to operate effectively. Call a meeting with your team and have each person write a sentence describing their role and the expectations associated with that role. Then share them throughout the team.

Be a Leader

Whether it's a small task or a year-long project, lead. Lead with your attitude, lead with your commitment to excellence, and lead with your unique perspective. Take stock of every activity your team performs. Find one area in which you can be the go-to person and make progress in that area.

Own Your Work

Create a culture of accountability by owning everything you do. If you're a manager, be accountable for your team. If you're a team member, own your role and your tasks. A culture of accountability garners respect and powers high level work.

CHAPTER 11

Team Growth and Expansion

By Brittany Drury

Did any of your first days on a job entail walking into a new role, excited to get started, only to be given six hours of mandatory trainings and paperwork with a small group lunch squeezed in?

Nearly 90 percent of new employees decide whether to stay with a new employee within their first six months on the job,[1] and this decision is influenced by their first days, weeks, and months of onboarding. Moreover, a study by the Wynhurst Group indicates that employees who experience a structured onboarding process are 58 percent more likely to remain with that organization after three years[2]—58 percent! Research and experience show that investing immediately and sincerely in each new hire's experience also correlates to their own expectations of performance and achievement. The key to building, retaining, and expanding a high-performing team begins with a high-performing system for onboarding, integrating, and investing in each new hire. Yet, all too often, a thoughtful onboarding process can easily take a back seat to deadlines and competing priorities.

As a team grows, it can become increasingly difficult to maintain consistency in performance and team culture, especially with the prevalence of dispersed remote teams. However, a robust onboarding process can increase new hire retention by 82 percent and boost productivity by 70 percent.[3] Just as a quality operating system enables a global franchise to rapidly scale its footprint while consistently delivering on its product and brand promise, a well-defined onboarding system is paramount to unlock your team's ability to expand without diminishing its culture or performance.

It's time we prioritize the employees' onboarding experiences and earn the right to retain the hyper-performers we work so hard to hire. This chapter will position you with the tools to do just that!

Build Your System

Take Time to Develop an Effective Onboarding System: It's One of the Most Critical Investments You Will Make

As our team explored doubling our size over a six-month period, we knew we needed a better system to scale talent. Until this point, we had grown slowly and organically. We developed successful onboarding practices, but many were implicit. Our process was not formally documented or accessible, and only a few members had an end-to-end understanding, placing a disproportionate burden on them and limiting our ability to leverage the full team in the process. Our fragmented approach burdened those who were responsible for guiding a new hire's onboarding experience. They had to piece together content, tools, and best practices by talking to multiple team members. It also created ambiguity for new team members who were not able to effectively gauge their progress against a baseline. There had to be a better way!

The high-performance onboarding system laid out in this chapter is the product of nearly two years of team research, ideation, experimentation, and iteration with proven results. This new system has unlocked our team's scalability, reduced the time required to prepare for a new hire from 60 hours to 3 hours—a nearly 95 percent time reduction—and received overwhelming praise from new teammates who've called the experience effortless, immersive, action-based, connected, and caring.

> In over ten years of working in the technology industry, my new hire onboarding experience on the Fusion team has, by far, exceeded every job I've ever had. Even before I officially started my first day, I felt set up for success and connected to my new colleagues. The care and attention paid to the onboarding process is a direct reflection of how we treat our customers.
>
> —Kelly Miller, Fusion

A high-caliber onboarding system has four key components:

1. **Talent Blueprint:** the end-to-end strategy and process to systematically find, onboard, guide, and retain exceptional talent
2. **Launchpad:** a collaborative learning platform that enables new hires to rapidly learn, integrate, and begin delivering value
3. **Sticky Moments:** special, celebratory moments embedded throughout the onboarding experience to create "stickiness" that retains newly hired talent
4. **Onboarding Mentor:** a guide, coach, and cheerleader who supports the new hire's success through their first 90 days

In the following sections of this chapter, we'll examine the importance of each component, how to begin building and integrating each of them into your own processes and provide visual templates to get you well on your way to attracting and retaining top-notch talent.

> **Reflect:** Before you start, reflect on your current onboarding process. Do you have a consistent or ad-hoc approach? Is the process explicit or implied?

Component 1: Talent Blueprint

Map to Learn and Iterate Often

The Talent Blueprint (Figure 11.1) creates the visibility and transparency your team needs to scale effectively. By articulating the Why, How, and What elements of each onboarding phase, you'll gain a detailed understanding of the current onboarding process, and how it can be improved.

The Talent Blueprint is an iterative artifact that describes the vision, approach, and end-to-end processes for identifying and retaining new talent. Think of it as both a living source of truth as well as a workspace for innovation. Your initial Talent Blueprint draft should explore the current state onboarding process and experience. The objective is to learn! Once the current state is understood, make a conscious practice of experimenting with new ideas and iterating often to continuously improve the Blueprint.

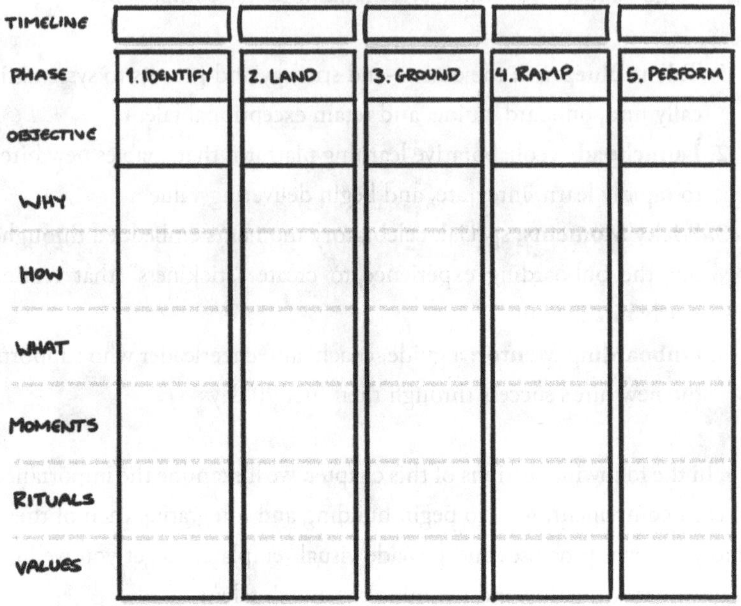

TIMELINE					
PHASE	1. IDENTIFY	2. LAND	3. GROUND	4. RAMP	5. PERFORM
OBJECTIVE					
WHY					
HOW					
WHAT					
MOMENTS					
RITUALS					
VALUES					

Figure 11.1 Talent Blueprint framework

Step 1: Define the Superstructure

The first step is to identify the superstructure (Figure 11.2) of your talent acquisition and development process. To start, it can be helpful to think about the "bookends" of your Talent Blueprint. These are the entry and exit points of your end-to-end onboarding experience. Be sure to build your blueprint as far upstream into the talent acquisition process as your team is involved. With these bookends in mind, determine the key **phases** that define a new hire's journey from talent identification to full team integration. Specify the expected **timeline** for progression and key **objectives** for each phase.

Step 2: Go Deeper on Each Phase

With the superstructure in place, identify the Why, How, and What elements for each phase (see Figure 11.2, Phase 4 for examples). These should each be detailed and explicit:

- **Why:** the belief underpinning your team's methods for accomplishing the objective of each phase

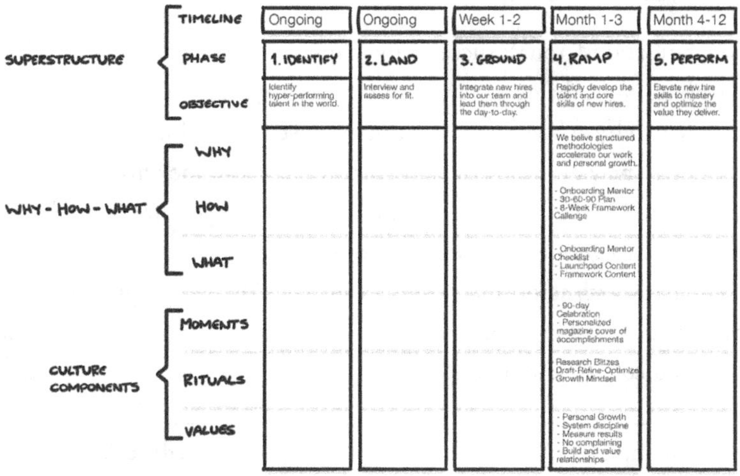

		Ongoing	Ongoing	Week 1-2	Month 1-3	Month 4-12
SUPERSTRUCTURE	TIMELINE					
	PHASE	1. IDENTIFY	2. LAND	3. GROUND	4. RAMP	5. PERFORM
	OBJECTIVE	Identify hyper-performing talent in the world.	Interview and assess for fit.	Integrate new hires into our team and lead them through the day-to-day.	Rapidly develop the talent and core skills of new hires.	Elevate new hire skills to mastery and optimize the value they deliver.
WHY – HOW – WHAT	WHY				We belive structured methodologies accelerate our work and personal growth.	
	HOW				- Onboarding Mentor - 30-60-90 Plan - 8-Week Framework Challenge	
	WHAT				- Onboarding Mentor Checklist - Launchpad Content - Framework Content	
CULTURE COMPONENTS	MOMENTS				- 90-day Celebration - Personalized magazine cover of accomplishments	
	RITUALS				Research Blitzes Draft-ReVise-Optimize Growth Mindset	
	VALUES				- Personal Growth - System discipline - Measure results - No complaining - Build and value relationships	

Figure 11.2 Talent Blueprint example: Superstructure, Why-How-What, and Culture Components

- **How:** the methods used to accomplish the objective
- **What:** the breakdown of steps necessary for each method to succeed, including artifacts and tools that support success

Next, consider the cultural components—**Sticky Moments, Rituals,** and **Values**—that reinforce the objective and Why in each phase of the onboarding experience (see Figure 11.2, Phase 4 for examples).

1. **Sticky Moments:** memorable moments, intentionally designed to foster belonging, build connection, and instill devotion to the team. More on this later in the chapter!
2. **Team Rituals:** the implicit or explicit practices that reinforce team values. Team rituals should be introduced to new hires early and reinforced throughout each phase. Exposing candidates to team rituals during the interview process gives them a feel for your team's ethos and whether they would be a good fit. For a deep dive into creating and adopting team rituals, see Chapter 7, "Intentional Communication."
3. **Team Values:** the principles that guide a team's behavior, attitude, collaboration, and performance. For more on Team Values, see Chapter 1, "Purpose, Passion, People."

Step 3: Learn and Improve

Congratulations! You've successfully mapped out your end-to-end talent blueprint. Now, the quest for improvement begins! Don't wait for an exit interview to learn how your team can improve its recruiting and onboarding; talk to new hires at regular intervals throughout the onboarding process to learn about their experiences. This will help you understand what they feel you're doing especially well and what could be done even better. External research across industries can also provide new insights and ideas for your onboarding experience. Test ideas with new hires, gather feedback, and continue to iterate.

> After mapping out your blueprint, stand back and **reflect**: What surprised you? Which opportunities stand out?

Component 2: The Launchpad

Onboarding in Action

When our team rapidly expanded and became fully remote, we had to rethink our in-office onboarding and training model to successfully ramp up new team members virtually. We needed to create a digital space that enabled new hires to feel connected and equipped to learn our craft. Thus, the Fusion Launchpad was born.

The *Launchpad* is a digital learning space that provides all the tools a new hire needs to:

- Discover team culture.
- Master the craft.
- Deliver unlimited value.

It enables your team to successfully scale its talent by consistently ramping new hires into rockstar contributors in record time. Every time.

Follow the design examples throughout this chapter to build your team's Launchpad template. We recommend building it in a collaborative virtual whiteboard application like Miro or Mural. A digital collaboration space like this simplifies the new hire experience with one space for all

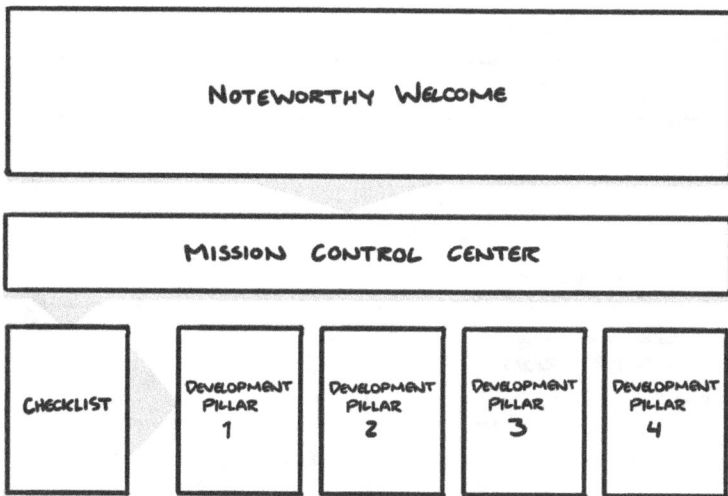

Figure 11.3 Launchpad framework

onboarding information. It provides visibility to the onboarding mentor and the hiring manager, which is important for remote teams. Once you've designed a template for your team, duplicate and personalize it to create a consistent onboarding workspace for each new team member.

The Launchpad consists of three key sections (Figure 11.3):

1. **Noteworthy Welcome**: a personalized welcome with an overview of Day 1, Week 1, and the team, as well as optional deep dives to learn about the team and organization
2. **Mission Control Center**: a dashboard to plan development goals and track progress
3. **Checklist and Development Pillars**: a space where intentional skill development, learning, and knowledge transfer take place

Noteworthy Welcome

The purpose of the *Noteworthy Welcome* section (Figure 11.4) is to:

- Make the new hire feel valued and at ease.
- Convey your team's excitement and eager anticipation of the new hire's arrival.

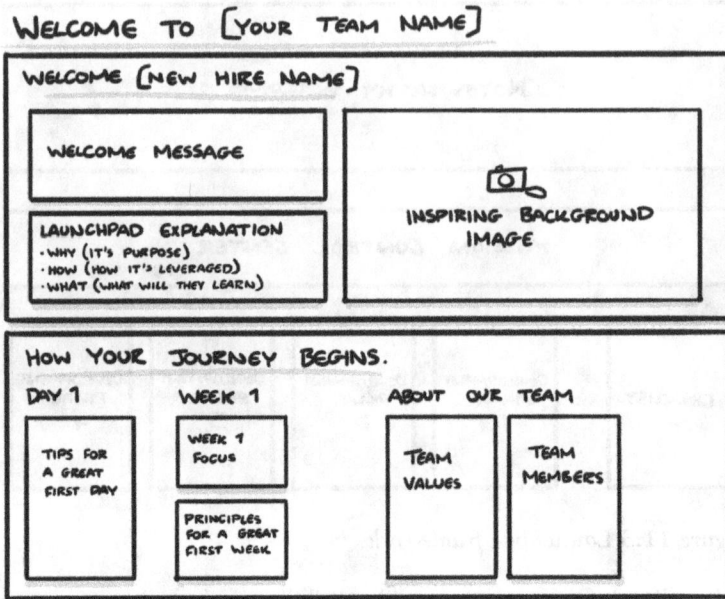

Figure 11.4 Launchpad: Noteworthy Welcome section

- Provide just enough high-level information to mitigate the
  new hire's anxiety on their first day.

The Noteworthy Welcome is the face of your team and company and
influences the new hire's first impressions. Ensure it accurately represents
your team's personality and brand. Provide access to the Launchpad prior
to the start date so they can get answers to some of the questions they
may have. To avoid overwhelming the new hire with information, the
Noteworthy Welcome is the only section of the Launchpad that is shared
with the new hire prior to their start date.

Your Noteworthy Welcome should include the following key elements:
- Personalized welcome message
- Brief explanation of the Launchpad
- An overview of how the new hire's journey will begin
  - Day 1
    - Tips for a great first day
  - Week 1
    - Week 1 focus

- Principles for a great first week
- Information about your team
  - Team Values
  - Team members; For each team member, include their headshot, email, phone number, and a link to their LinkedIn page.
- Optional exploration; Link topics to more detailed material. Below are topics our new hires have found most valuable.
  - **Who are we?** *Learn about our team's business offerings.*
  - **Communicating what we do:** *How to explain your new role to friends and family.*
  - **How we like to work:** *Learn about our team's working style.*
  - **Daily routine:** *An overview of our weekly standup schedule.*
  - **Team wins!** *Highlights from our team's impact this year.*
  - **The organization:** *Learn how our team fits into the broader organizational ecosystem.*

Mission Control Center

The *Mission Control Center* section (Figure 11.5) is the persistent dashboard that the new hire, their onboarding mentor, and the hiring manager will use to:

- Plan and track development goals.
- Provide personal and team feedback.
- Easily access important resources through quick links.

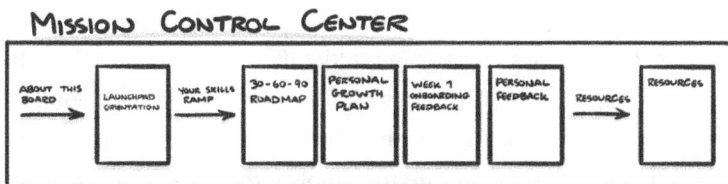

Figure 11.5 Launchpad: Mission Control Center section

Key elements of the Mission Control Center include:

- **30-60-90 Roadmap:** an outline of expected milestones the new hire will reach over the next 30, 60, and 90 days, including key deliverables, accomplishments, and any critical training certifications.
- **Onboarding feedback:** daily feedback the new hire provides to the team about their onboarding experience—framed in the form of Keepers and Improvers[4]
- **Personal feedback:** weekly feedback the onboarding mentor and team members working directly with the new hire provide—framed in the form of Keepers and Improvers.
- **Resources:** key resources to help the new hire build their knowledge base, including links to trusted resources to grow their industry-specific literacy, newsletters and blogs, acronym dictionaries, and even "words of wisdom" from previous teammates and interns who have been part of your team's journey—huge accelerators for early career individuals and those transitioning into a new industry.

Checklist and Development Pillars

Skill development, learning, and knowledge transfer take place in this section of the Launchpad. Each of the four development pillars (Figure 11.6) delivers distinct and complementary content for rapid skill development. We recommend grouping content into weekly themes across the pillars to reduce cognitive load. It can be helpful to include a corresponding weekly checklist for learnings and action items to help them determine where to begin and what to prioritize.

Pillar 1: Individual Tasks

These are discrete tasks to get the new hire up and running on the team! Include enough step-by-step instructions so the new hire can complete these tasks on their own. It may seem tedious to build out detailed instructions, but enabling the new hire to complete these tasks independently instills an early sense of accomplishment while unlocking the bandwidth

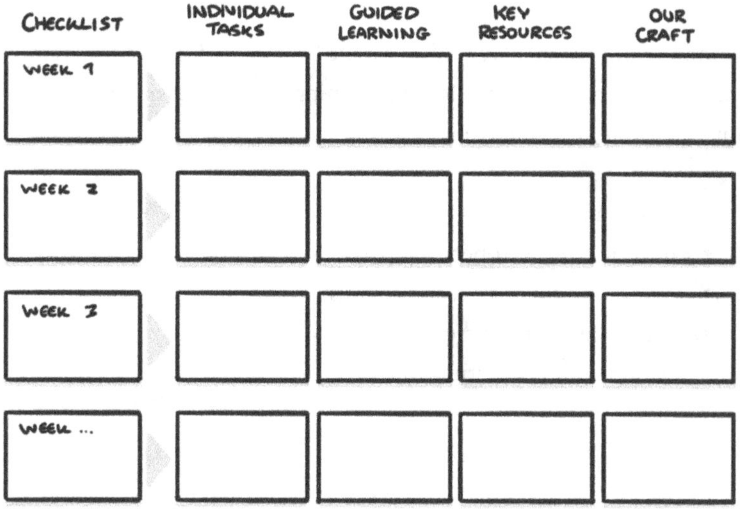

CHECKLIST	INDIVIDUAL TASKS	GUIDED LEARNING	KEY RESOURCES	OUR CRAFT
WEEK 1				
WEEK 2				
WEEK 3				
WEEK ...				

Figure 11.6 Launchpad: Checklist and Development Pillars section

of the onboarding mentor to take on additional work while fulfilling this role. Individual tasks may include:

- **IT checklist:** a step-by-step guide to get their workstation up and running.
- **Team one-on-one checklist:** include unique conversation starters for each team member, such as a specific area of expertise to inquire about, the history of the team, and so on.
- **Prospective resume:** a draft of what their future resume will reflect after their time on the team. Explicitly capturing what the new hire would like to accomplish can be an especially helpful exercise for interns, to ensure their time is well spent and mutually valuable.
- **Personal why:** a space to reflect on their own personal mission statement by exploring purpose, objective statements, goals, strategies, and measures (more in Chapter 1, "Purpose, Passion, People")
- **Elevator pitch:** a prewritten script for the new hire to internalize so they're equipped to confidently pitch a 30-second summary of your business, goals, and vision to colleagues and prospective clients

Pillar 2: Guided Learning

Guided Learnings are core topics that are best learned from a teacher who can guide the new hire through the learning and answer questions in real time. Learning topics may include:

- Team values and beliefs
- Team rituals and operating patterns
- Core tools, platforms, and portals
- Team operations and owners
- Daily standup structure

Pillar 3: Accelerators

Accelerators are key internal and external resources that augment and accelerate the new hire's individual tasks, guided learning, and training focus for the week. Including multiple forms of media can boost engagement with the material. Some accelerators we include are:

- Books
- Short videos
- Articles or whitepapers
- Original content produced by the team

Pillar 4: Training

Trainings focus on the skill development required for the new hire to ramp up on your team's craft. This section is comprised of self-study and guided learning. We've found it helpful to organize multiple modules into internal team certifications to help the new hire gauge how they're tracking on their journey to mastery. A few examples of our team's modules include:

- Self-Led Training
  - Fusion Fast-Pitch (elevator pitch)
  - Design Foundations

- Mentor-Led Training
  - Fast Facts Quizzes
  - 8-Week Framework Challenge
  - Hyperlearning
  - Mental Models

Reflect: How can you bolster a new hire's noteworthy welcome to make it representative of your team's unique brand identity?

Component 3: Sticky Moments

Make It Human: Create Special Moments That Drive Stickiness

We often focus on the need to delight customers but forget that delighting team members also creates significant value return. Building a collection of positive, standout memories—*sticky moments*—into the new hire's experience fosters belonging, builds connection, and instills devotion to the team. Sticky moments are milestone occasions that stand out across the end-to-end experience.

Think of interesting and innovative ways to make new hire milestones—like contract signing, Day 1, and the 90-day mark—standout moments worth remembering.

In their book, *The Power of Moments*, authors Chip and Dan Health tell us that the most memorable moments are created by incorporating four key elements:

1. **Elevation:** creating memorable delight and breaking the script
2. **Insight:** defining moments that change how we view ourselves or the world
3. **Pride:** spontaneous recognition of achievement
4. **Connection:** deepening ties by experiencing the moment together[5]

Below are a few ideas our team has used to effectively turn each milestone into a sticky moment.

Contract Signing

After the hiring contract is confirmed, we send two celebratory welcome packages to the new hire to give them a sense of our team and our values. Investing in this sticky moment early on demonstrates how much we value them joining our team at a critical time when the new hire may still be receiving other offers.

- Package 1: a set of books that our team feels are intrinsic to our team values, practices, and the everyday work that we do
- Package 2: sweet treats that represent some of the things our team of foodies enjoys (brownies, cookies, coffee, etc.)

We also make a conscious effort to purchase the contents of these packages from local and minority-owned businesses. Some retailers may donate a portion of the sales from a purchase to a charity of choice, in which case, we've directed the donation to the charity of the new hire's choice. In these smaller intentional practices, we're able to demonstrate early on how important it is for us to positively impact the world, even through small actions.

First Day

- We create a personalized "welcome doodle" (hand-drawn by one of our designers) for the new hire. During our morning standup, we *elevate* the new hire's first meeting with the team by having each team member set the welcome doodle as their virtual backgrounds, demonstrating that each of us are cheerleaders for the new hire's success and happy to have them aboard.
- We host a couple of small group lunches to build *connections* between the new hire and the team. We find that the smaller group format is a little less overwhelming and creates a more conducive, low-pressure atmosphere for the new hire to get to know the other team members as well as more time for organic conversation. We encourage everyone to have their lunch delivered and expensed to ensure it is an inclusive and welcoming moment, regardless of their location.

90-Day Mark

- We *elevate* our gratitude by having each team member send a personalized e-mail to congratulate the new team member and synchronize them to be delivered at the same time for an extra wow factor.
- We build *pride* by dedicating our team standup meetings to listen to the new team member's wisdom—what surprised them about our team and what they have learned over their first 90 days.
- We inspire *connection* by presenting the new hire with a "90-day Gratitude Collage" that showcases their contributions to our various chat threads, as well as personal notes from each teammate on why they love working with the new team member and their favorite memorable moment with them.
- We instill *pride* by designing a faux magazine cover that features the new team member. We select a magazine cover that is personally meaningful to them, often relating to their favorite pastimes or hobbies (e.g., sports, travel, gaming, running) to show that we've learned about what's important to them and who they are as a human. The stories featured on the cover celebrate their hard work and everything they've accomplished in their first 90 days.
- We *elevate* the new team member's 90th day by booking it with pseudo meetings, which suddenly disappear when their manager tells them to take the day off.

> **Reflect:** Which moments of your current onboarding experience truly stand out? Where is there an opportunity to bolster stickiness?

Component 4: Onboarding Mentor

Your New Hire's Cheerleader, Coach, and Life Jacket

The value and importance of an onboarding mentor, who serves as a single point of contact for the new hire, cannot be understated. According to *Harvard Business Review*, research from a pilot of 600 employees at

Microsoft found that a formal onboarding mentor accelerates new hires in three fundamental ways: [6]

1. **Context:** Onboarding mentors can make important contextual connections for new hires by teaching them about team values, rituals, and cultural norms that are often more implicit in nature. They can also make a conscious effort to build the new hire's network outside of the team by introducing them to at least one new organizational leader each week, and helping the new hire understand and navigate the organizational structure.

2. **Productivity:** One-on-one mentorship provides new hires with the dedicated direction and support they need to ramp up their skills, push beyond their comfort zone, and rapidly achieve growth and productivity. Onboarding mentors should prioritize one-on-one time with the new hire and ensure a consistent cadence. Microsoft's pilot showed a strong positive correlation between the number of times that the new hire met with their onboarding mentor and the new hire's perception of their speed to productivity (Figure 11.7).

3. **Satisfaction:** Mentors also play an important role in building a sense of friendship and connection with the team, a key aspect of satisfaction with, and connection to, the broader company. When asked about their onboarding experience after their first week, new hires with onboarding mentors were 23 percent more satisfied than those without mentors. Moreover, new hire satisfaction continued to grow, reaching a 36 percent increase in satisfaction after 90 days. These findings are echoed across industry research. UrbanBound reports that "70 percent of employees say that friends at work is the most crucial element to a happy working life."[7] And organizational psychologist, Dr. Jan West, says that employee satisfaction skyrockets nearly 50 percent when a worker develops a close relationship at work.[8]

With all this data backing the effectiveness of mentorship, what can we do to ensure that the onboarding mentor relationship is a positive experience for both parties?

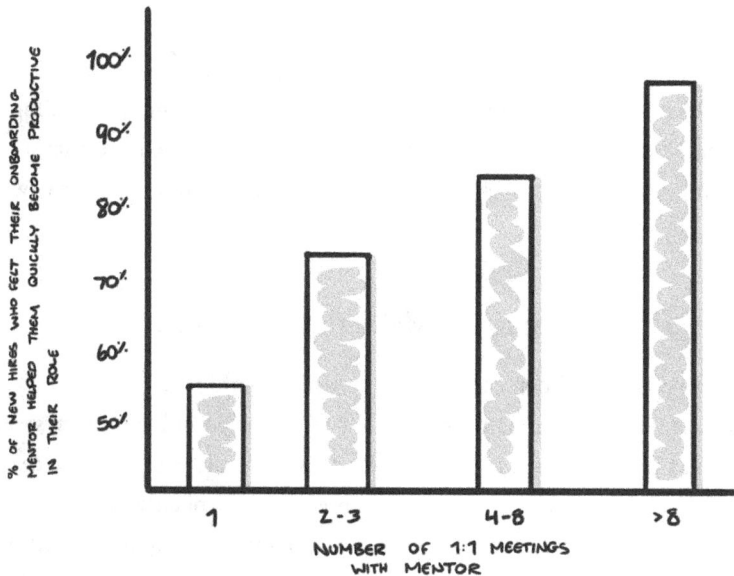

Figure 11.7 *Impact of mentor meetings on new hire perspection of speed to productivity (at 90 days)*[6]

- Formalize the mentor's relationship with the new hire. Be clear about the duration of this relationship and the expectations of mentorship.
- Ensure the mentor possesses the following qualities: They should be a champion of your organizational culture and have deep knowledge of the team, company, and new hire's role. Ideally, the mentor would be on the same team and reporting to the same manager as the new hire.
- Be cognizant of the mentor's workload. The mentor should have enough bandwidth to prioritize the experience and needs of the new hire. If they cannot, consider shifting the mentor's workload to another teammate or appointing a different individual to mentor. (See Chapter 3, "Inclusion and Diversity" for deeper perspectives on mentorship through an I&D lens.)
- Introduce the mentor and new hire prior to Day 1. Include the mentor's personal information (e-mail and phone). A

lifeline like this can reduce the new hire's stress level going into Day 1.

> **Reflect:** Which of your team members embody strong onboarding mentor qualities? What steps do you need to take to ensure that all team members can develop these qualities to successfully mentor new hires?

Get Started: Make the Investment

Employers lose 17 percent of their new hires within their first 90 days due to ineffective onboarding.[9] With a finely tuned onboarding system as your secret weapon, you will retain talent and scale your team successfully. The time to amp up your game is now. Begin explicitly mapping out your end-to-end onboarding experience and adopt a systematic method to continuously improve it. Take steps to develop a truly memorable onboarding experience and ramping machine for your new hires. It will deepen their commitment to the team and their work, and ultimately accelerate their ability to create value.

Think back to your own experience starting a new job and how hard it was to be productive and comfortable with a new team and a new company. Now, imagine a transformed onboarding experience that:

- Enabled you to enter your first day feeling highly valued and deeply connected to your team
- Explicitly laid out your path to success
- Paired you with a mentor who accelerated your learning, and
- Created moments to celebrate your achievements

Imagine an experience where you could drive value and feel reaffirmed with that same feeling you had when you first took the job—that this is where you belong.

Key Takeaways

Take Your First Step. Make Exceptional Onboarding an Explicit Team Priority.

Map Your Talent Blueprint

Begin exploring the current state onboarding process and experience. Allocate an hour to map out your blueprint superstructure. Schedule time with teammates to gain a comprehensive understanding of the current state (Why, How, What, Rituals, Moments, and Values).

Build Your Launchpad

Research and select a virtual collaboration/whiteboarding platform for your Launchpad.

Create Sticky Moments

Prioritize opportunities to make new hire milestones moments worth remembering. Identify one sticky moment and adapt it for a recent (or upcoming!) new hire.

Formalize Onboarding Mentors

Formalize the mentoring relationship between the new hire and the mentor. Outline the onboarding mentor's role. Include expectations of both mentor and mentee, as well as the role's duration to ensure a positive experience for everyone.

PART 3

Creating Massive Value

Jigsaw Pieces

By Lianza Reyes

one tiny part to the entire whole
doesn't seem much to accomplish the goal
take the other parts, see where they fit
see what happens when the team can commit
see what you can picture you can generate.
and then find the questions you want to accelerate.
the jigsaw picture is never the final solution
it's the spark that puts a journey into motion
you ask, what should the picture have? what does it need?
then you chase the steps in order to succeed.
from the jigsaw comes a grander scene,
and the actions that you had pursued in between.
you find the passion to love what you do,
and from this discovery is to *create value*.

PART 5

Creating Massive Value

Jigsaw Pieces

By Lianaa Reyes

CHAPTER 12

Creating Massive Value

By Shane Picciotto

"My internship at Kaiser was canceled because of Covid-19," a nursing student said. It was April 2020 and internships were in short supply due to the global pandemic, and internships were a prerequisite for this nurse to finish school. I considered ways I might help her: on our team and throughout the company we were in a hiring freeze, and I was preoccupied with supporting a workshop to help clients align their goals. It would take about four hours of my time to talk with my boss and complete the process to submit the internship for approval from Finance.

During that day and over the following week, I leaned on some of my teammates and pushed out work that could wait to make time to submit the internship. We were really just looking to help someone out because, after the time invested to ramp an intern, we're lucky to break even with the value the intern is able to create directly for the team. However, just as Bill Gates has reflected that "There are two great forces in human nature: self-interest, and caring for others,"[1] our team similarly believes that a value-first mindset applied to the benefit of others and not the self results in greater value realization for all. There are four key principles that make a value-first mindset easy to follow. They all provide boundaries and constraints to help you give more freely and create greater value realization overall.

1. Balance selfishness with selflessness;
2. Short-term benefit is short-sighted.
3. Solve for the root cause, not the symptom.
4. Steal like an artist or create on your own.

Principle 1: Balance Selfishness with Selflessness

The first principle, balancing selfishness with selflessness, helps counteract our natural and systemic tendencies. There is a lot of pressure to be selfish: We get paid to go to work and create value for our team. And, if you work in a company larger than 100+ people, you're likely not getting paid to help others outside of your team. You are definitely not getting paid to help those outside of the company. Conversely, there are a lot of pressures to be selfless. We want to help people that are older or younger than us, or those that do not enjoy the privileges we do. It's part of being human. We wouldn't have the companies, communities, and nations we do today without a large dose of selflessness.

There's a healthy tension between selfishness and selflessness and each individual must balance that in different ways over time. For our team, there are some weeks when we're more selfless, and we help those in our community or support the company's talent development programs. Other weeks require focus on client work, and we turn down opportunities to help others.

Principle 2: Short-Term Benefit Is Short-Sighted

When focusing on short-term benefits, we often miss out on other opportunities. If you think about your time as the primary resource you use to create value, then we should be thinking about our time investments with a portfolio approach. People who are out to maximize the returns on their financial assets don't invest the majority of their funds in money markets or bonds. And yet, that's what we try to do when we think about whether or not something is a worthwhile investment. Focusing solely on short-term benefits is short-sighted.

What we should be doing when thinking about helping others and creating value is a portfolio investment. A portfolio investment spreads risk across several different types of investments to help someone achieve their financial goals. If your goal is to retire in the next year, you had better make sure most of your assets are in cash, bonds, or something similar. However, for most of us, we want to have investments across a much broader spectrum. We also want to keep those investments long enough to yield a return.

Here's what our portfolio investment looks like at the team level:

- Core Work
- Engagements
- Atomic Hours

Our team's **core work** is to help the enterprise we work within identify and solve problems they will face three months from now. 60 percent of our work focuses on defining these obstacles through projects we call sessions. The impact is high, and the probability of success is high as well.

We consider work that takes place over a longer period of time—months not weeks—to be more of an **engagement**. The impact is medium to high, and the probability of success is medium to high.

Atomic Hours were created by our team as a means to keep our consulting abilities and knowledge sharp. They are 5 percent of our total time—helping anyone that needs it, like a start-up, local nonprofit, or a student group. Atomic Hours take an hour or two of a teammate's day and are highly dynamic, so they require little additional preparation apart from scheduling the meeting itself. These are high impact but lower probability of success projects.

In order to develop and apply an investor's mindset to managing your time, involve your full team to understand the types of work your team engages in and when the likely return can be expected. It's difficult for most of us to assess the potential outcomes of our work without bias. Asking multiple people across your team (or a board of directors, if you have one) will get you what you need without causing over-analysis on your part. Applying the principle of this section, the short-term benefit is short-sighted, ensuring that you're creating value that's not just easy and safe. Instead of taking the comfortable path, you'll be pushing yourself to create value even where it feels risky. Helping the nurse who was looking for an internship is a great example. There wasn't a lot of hiring going on when I said I would look into it and submit the job requisition—it could have jeopardized future hires that we wanted to make, but we took the uncomfortable path.

Principle 3: Solve for the Root Cause, Not the Symptom

When looking to find the right place to gain insight from others, another avenue that we've often found helpful is to do a root cause analysis. A root cause analysis looks to identify the cause behind a given problem. It's much more art than science because the only science is asking "why?" until you find the processes or human behaviors underlying the problem. Once you reach that point, you can make a lasting change.

Several years ago, we worked with a client who was looking to understand how they could decrease the time nurses spent on administrative work. The nurses see six to eight patients a day inside the patients' homes and work as a team. Previously, they worked late nights looking up patient information for the next day and making calls to confirm and reassure patients they would see them.

One of the problems communicated was that patients often rescheduled their appointments the day before. The first feedback we received was that patients forgot they had a visit the next day. However, when you drill down to the root by asking "Why?" we saw that the actual causes were that patients were often uncomfortable having someone come inside their home, they were nervous about receiving a more severe diagnosis, or they wanted to see the nurse they had visited the time before.

Once you've found the root cause, you can then find others who have solved the problem. However, not all problem-solvers are created equal. For solving problems related to product management, you might look at blogs from thought leaders such as John Cutler, Andresen Horowitz, or Steve Blank. Next, you could look at organizations such as 280 Group and Pragmatic Marketing which conduct training for product managers. Our team relies on three different sources:

1. **Consulting firms** such as McKinsey, Bain, and Accenture
2. **Leading companies** such as Apple, Google, and Spotify
3. **Institutions** such as the Harvard Business Review, Stanford, and INSEAD

Start taking action and look for others who you might gain inspiration from. Build a list and add to it as you solve other problems. Ask a few good team members to help you make short work of an otherwise daunting task. When solving a problem for the first time and inspiration from a variety of sources is needed, we often conduct a Research Blitz as a team. By leveraging the collective focus of our team to research a given topic simultaneously and compile a large volume of information that jumpstarts our fellow teammates in solving the problem at hand. In addition to the breadth of information that is uncovered, we also benefit from team insights and perspectives along the way that we'd otherwise be unlikely to discover. It's like watching a game from multiple different seats in a stadium, all at the same time. You get a better perspective than if you were trying to find inspiration and solutions all on your own.

Principle 4: Steal Like an Artist or Create on Your Own

The third principle has two parts: steal like an artist or create on your own.

Steal Like an Artist

We all have jobs because we're trying to solve a problem, whether that's packaging something to be shipped, creating an information technology strategy, or identifying a new way to delight customers. Every problem is unique, but it's unlikely that the problem is so unique that you can't find inspiration from another source. Mark Twain once said, "History doesn't repeat itself, but if often rhymes." We should learn from history and be unashamed about doing so. Rather than trying to solve a problem all on our own, we should be open to seeing how someone else solved the problem and learn from how they did it.

"If you were to read every book in the Library of Congress, it would take you 18,000 years of nonstop reading."[2]

When trying to solve a problem that is very tactical, you often need to look at close examples to solve it. The more broad, abstract, or general your problem is, the further afield you must go to solve it. For example, when our team was engaged to help call center agents increase their customer satisfaction scores, we were able to draw inspiration from many industries: hospitality, amusement parks, and leading technology companies. There are a lot of dimensions to a problem that large, and we could get inspiration from many different sources to solve that problem. However, if we're seeking to understand how we could increase engagement during the monthly town hall meetings, the problem is more constrained and would require us to look at closer examples for inspiration—such as how other teams inside our enterprise have succeeded in increasing their engagement, how universities keep their students engaged, or how other companies communicate broad messages to their teams.

It's important to avoid confusing problem size and solution size when looking at historical examples or how others have solved the problem. If you have a big problem, you don't necessarily need a big solution. For example, take the call center team we just talked about. If the call center team were looking to improve their Net Promoter Score (NPS)[3], they don't need to train and work at the Ritz Carlton for six months to learn about leading world-class teams. That would be a large-sized solution to a large problem. Instead, they could do something as simple as sharing best practices at a regular frequency amongst internal teams. A big problem does NOT equal a big solution.

Create on Your Own

Attention is a scarce resource. It's something that seems straightforward, but in today's economy where attention is at a premium, it's often hard to find time to do just that. However, attention and focus are required to create great work.

Creating something requires focus and, in the modern world, there are many powerful forces seeking that focus. From trivial social media to the seemingly important tasks like checking e-mail hourly, it is not easy to create a space to focus. There are a couple of methods our team uses to improve focus.

The first way is to send a clear message that we don't want to be interrupted, such as putting in headphones. Those headphones can be virtual like a "do not disturb" status on a messaging application, or simply closing a chat. The Fusion team has many people in-office and I've often found myself putting headphones in, without actually plugging them into an audio device.

A second method to create greater focus and, thus, greater productivity, is by timeboxing your work. There are many methods to do so. One that we use is called the Pomodoro Technique. There are three steps:

1. Set a goal.
2. Focus your work on this goal, undisturbed, for 25–90 minutes.
3. Reward yourself.

Keeping others from breaking your focus is relatively easy with headphones and do-not-disturb messages. Keeping *yourself* from being disturbed is much more difficult. Some people go to a specific location where they only do focused work. Some have a ritual before they start working to help get their mind into focus. Each person will have different techniques and tactics to help them create their focus.

A commonly overlooked aspect of creating focus is setting a reward at the end of your accomplishment. Our brains release chemicals that help us focus when we know that we're anticipating a reward at the end. That reward could be a walk, a conversation with a colleague, checking a blog, or getting a snack. The specifics don't matter but, to be effective, it must be something that you look forward to. The reward I set when I helped the nurse with an internship was a ten-minute walk around a local park—a chance for me to stretch my legs, get some fresh air, and boost my own brain power at the same time.

We began the chapter by talking about the intern that we hired without expecting any significant return. Fast forward three months to the end of the summer: she became a key member of the team and created a clinical leadership model to help retain clinicians in our organization— all while using the three value-first principles to create the model. First, she *balanced selfishness with selflessness* by working on this program in her time that wasn't directly allocated to client work. Second, she *focused on the longer-term benefit* this program would provide because, by the time the clinical program kicked off, she had completed her internship and was already back in school. And third, she *solved the root cause, not the problem*, by going to the source, interviewing clinicians in the field, and drilling deeply to discover the underlying drivers of clinician burnout and attrition. And last, she embodied *create on your own*, or *steal like an artist*, by looking at best-in-class leadership programs across the country. A great example of how a value-first mindset applied to the benefit of others— not the self—results in greater value realization for all. She created value for herself, the Fusion team, and the broader enterprise.

Reflect: What steps can you take to shift from an "I and me" to a "we and us" mindset?

Key Takeaways

Seize Opportunities for Rapid Value Creation

If you can help someone out in five minutes, do it even if you're not going to directly benefit.

Evaluate Your Efforts

Write down what you do each month, inside and outside of work. Are you focusing on short-term gains or taking a portfolio approach?

Practice Timeboxing

Set a timer when you're looking to do work, no fewer than 25 minutes, no more than 120, and most importantly, reward yourself at the end.

Collect Resources for Inspiration

Make a list of companies or previous projects from your team that you can steal from.

CHAPTER 13

Value-Based Marketing System

By Alexa Colyer

*Building marketing systems based on the value you provide your customers enables a **zero-lift ecosystem** of content creation, communication, and brand equity. Your team's marketing is driven from the actions you take to create value for others. Your team is a brand—you must **build it**, **defend it**, and **enable it**.*

If you are self-employed, an individual contributor, or a leader of a small- to mid-size team who wants to understand the importance of the value you and your team generate and how that builds your value-based marketing system, then this chapter is for you.

There is a high probability you don't have the resources, capacity, or funds to have a large marketing team. What you *do* have is dedication and drive to increase the value you and your team bring to your audience. Knowing how to support your team in the creation and execution of its brand will accelerate you on the path to a successful and manageable value-based marketing system.

Throughout this chapter, we will embrace the startup mindset. Everything we do must have a purpose and bring value. The outcome: You will walk away from this chapter with a deep understanding of a value-based marketing system and specific next steps you and your team can take to achieve an elite brand.

Value-Based Marketing System

What Is a Value-Based Marketing System?

A value-based marketing system is rooted in bringing *value* to your customers rather than being driven by profit, sales, revenue, and so on. When crafting your value-based marketing system, you must understand how it will evolve over time and how that directly relates to the value you provide to your audience (see Figure 13.1). The value to your audience increases as your value-based marketing system matures through each phase.

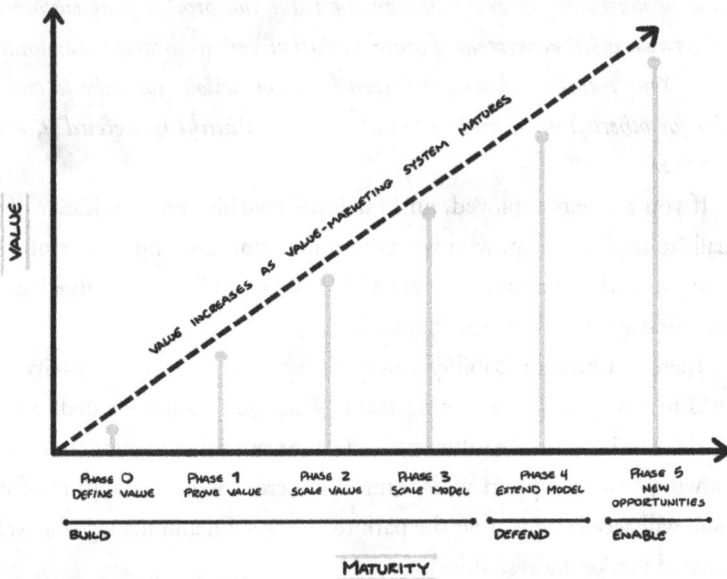

Figure 13.1 Phases of a value-based marketing system

As your marketing system matures, the value you bring to the world will increase.

Phase 0: **Define** the Value You Wish to Create (Build It)

As a team, define what type of value you will deliver to your audience and to the world. Are you offering a service, product, experience, or something else? How do you want to positively change or impact the lives of your intended audience?

Phase 1: **Prove** Your Value

How might you prove that you can quickly and efficiently deliver on the value you defined and promised?

Phase 2: **Scale** Your Value Hypothesis (Build It)

How might you scale that value and expand it to even more customers, people, audiences, and so on?

Phase 3: **Scale** the Model That Executes and Drives the Value (Build It)

Ensure your value delivery model can deliver on the additional value. How might you scale your value-based marketing system's processes?

Phase 4: **Extend** Your Model (Defend It)

How might you expand into new audiences or industries?

Phase 5: **Pursue** New Marketing and Value-Driven Milestones, Experiments, and Initiatives (Enable It)

The last phase allows your value-based marketing system to drive value on its own. Because you put in the work in the previous phases, you can pursue new opportunities to bring even greater value to your audience while your marketing system runs at scale.

Phase 0: Define the Value You Wish to Create (Build It)

Team Principles

Before you can provide value to your audience, you must understand and define *what* value you want to provide. A helpful starting point is identifying your team's principles. A team's principles are a list of statements that align team members. Everything your team produces and works on should align to the majority of your team's principles.

Team principles are also helpful when making team-wide decisions. For example, if a new opportunity comes along for your team to tackle and engage with, I encourage you to filter that opportunity through your team's principles. If it aligns to less than 25 percent of your team's principles, you should reconsider engaging in that opportunity. If it aligns to less than 25 percent of your team's principles but the team still wants to engage in the opportunity, perhaps you should revisit and evolve the principles themselves (although this is a rare instance).

Some examples of a team's principles are:

- Save our customers' time.
- Influence our employees.
- Fundamentally change how our customers work and live.

Allot dedicated time with your team to define these principles. It could take anywhere from 30 minutes to an hour to refine. What do you live by? What must hold true no matter what content you're publishing, the product you're bringing to the world, or the service you're offering? When defining your team's vision and principles, ensure you allow every team member to contribute. This ensures alignment with the final outputs and will accelerate the team when embracing the team's marketing system.

Your team's principles, for the most part, shouldn't change over time. You should stay true to your principles, even if the value, products, or services you're offering evolve or change. If necessary, principles can be added to or edited. If your principles do change, it's likely that your team's mission and its deeper, fundamental "why" may have evolved as well. You can learn more about the importance of finding your "why" in Chapter 1, "Purpose, Passion, People" and about building team principles in Chapter 9, "Elite Team Structure."

Example: Our Team's Phase 0

Our team began its value-based marketing journey at the very beginning when our team was first founded. We asked ourselves one simple question, and we continue to ask that question to this day: How might we bring value to every single employee in our company and the world?

Our team's vision statement is:

We empower teams to define a bold vision, get in the minds of users, and deliver products to market faster.

Some of our team's principles include:

- Accelerate key leaders across the globe toward their goals.
- Enable leaders to become market differentiators who craft powerful stories, structures, and strategies.
- Enable leaders to shift their practices from go-to, ordinary methods to the right tools and frameworks.

Through our vision statement and principles, we aligned our team of 20+ individuals to a common purpose. Even when we onboard new team members, which occurs multiple times a year, one of the first things we do is onboard them to our vision and principles.

From the very beginning, we knew our team was never going to follow a traditional sales model. It is true that when our team was first born, we had to pitch our vision and services to leaders throughout the company. However, the reason we pitched our team was to simply bring awareness to our team's purpose and mission rather than directly pitching our services.

At Phase 0, we also had support from one of our company's leaders. That leader was and, remains, invested in our success. Because this leader supported us, we had to deliver value to them first, and in doing so offered them first-hand experience of our ability to deliver value to the broader company.

Having someone outside of your team who can support you in your success is extremely beneficial. I encourage you to identify your champion or keep in mind who can eventually fulfill that role.

> **Reflect:** Who has supported you and your team since day one? Who aligns to your values, your vision statement, and your principles?

Vision Statement

A good first step in defining your team's brand is crafting and aligning to the team's vision statement. You may already have this defined. The difference here is crafting a *marketing* vision statement. The team's marketing vision statement should answer the questions: Why does your team care about marketing? What value are you providing to your audience?

A vision statement describes where the team aspires to be upon achieving its foundational why. You can think of the vision statement as the team's "why," which we discussed in Chapter 1, "Purpose, Passion, People."

A strong vision statement is:

- Future focused
- Directional
- Specific
- Relevant and purpose-driven
- Values-based
- Challenging
- Unique and memorable
- Inspiring

A vision statement describes where the company/team aspires to be upon achieving its foundational *why*. When constructing your vision statement, walk through these prompts:

- Who are your target customers?
- What is needed or what is the opportunity area?
- What is your product category? What are you doing differently?
- What is your key benefit? What is the most compelling reason to buy or use?
- What is the primary alternative or current-state system?
- What is your primary differentiator or the advantages of your product/approach?

For example, Patagonia's vision statement is "Build the best product, cause no unnecessary harm, use business to inspire and implement solutions to the environmental crisis."[1]

Phase 1: Prove Your Value (Build It)

Now that you have identified your team's principles, the next phase is to begin to prove your value and show your customers how you execute your principles. It is critical you only provide your audience with valuable, high-quality content, especially in this phase. When you are in the process of proving your value, you can't risk putting something into the world that might lack value to your customers. Everything they encounter with your team's name must be your best work.

When proving your value, try to engage with new (or existing) customers in ways that align to your team's vision statement and principles. If you're struggling to find folks to say yes to your offering, research the market or industry you're serving. What public content can you release that will bring value to others within your industry? How can you create traction through the content you're producing and gain new customers and audience members?

Throughout your entire marketing journey, feel free to get creative. Besides creating value through the services and products you offer, what other ways can you produce content? Perhaps you can write an article about a hot topic within your industry or send out a weekly e-mail to your leaders summarizing the valuable work you delivered that week.

Example: Our Team's Phase 1

To prove the value we wanted to bring to our company, our team started supporting and accelerating teams within a specific department. We focused on one offering: bringing teams together to tap into the combined potential of business, experience, technology, and user-centered design to improve the value of business systems and to deliver a go-forward strategy.

We engaged with teams by helping them build out roadmaps, user experiences, and future state journeys. At this stage, we did not have a well-formed process for engaging with teams. We operated under a rapid experimentation strategy, iterating with each opportunity and delivering on our clients' goals as we were asked.

We also heard "no thanks"—*a lot*. We needed to prove why others in our company should say "yes" to working with us. If you think of it from their perspective, here was this new two-person team asking if they could help another team solve a problem they were facing and accelerate them toward success. Without past clients and successful engagements, it was tricky to get someone to understand why engaging with our team would be beneficial to them. If we could get just *one* team to work with us and see the power behind our offerings, we could leverage that success to approach other teams.

Rather than wait for that first client, we produced high-value artifacts we anticipated would be attractive to leaders. We sent this content out in accordance with our principles—we knew we could help and chose to do so. Engaging in this manner enabled us to gain experience and feedback and build our portfolio by homing in on delivering value to our community. Pendo marketing leader, Joe Chernov, says "Good marketing makes the company look smart. Great marketing makes the customer feel smart."[2] We similarly found that the more value we generated and shared, the more we started to hear requests for our help. That led us into Phase 2.

Reflect: What value can you bring to your customers *now*? What pain points can you resolve for them to prove your value? How can you make their lives better?

Phase 2: Scale Your Value Hypothesis (Build It)

How might you bring even more value to your customers? This is a good time to ensure that everyone on your team is actively promoting and executing your value-based marketing system. Creating cohesion amongst your team is critical to the success of a value-based marketing system.

Having a consistent brand, vision statement, principles, and so on. across your team creates cohesion amongst team members. Everyone on the team should be able to naturally embrace that they are a promoter of the team's brand and the value the team is bringing to their customers. More importantly, everyone on the team should feel *proud* to represent the team's brand.

Creating a value-based marketing system for your team enables team members to feel empowered to provide value to your audience. When the entire team feels responsible for, and empowered by the team's brand and marketing system, the system runs itself. Yes, you will need someone to lead and drive the strategy, but the entire team will create content that is aligned to the team's brand.

This cohesion, unification, and empowerment across the team allows your team to scale its value hypothesis. In Phases 0 and 1, your team aligned to team principles and a marketing vision statement and began to form your value hypothesis: What and how you will bring the most value to your customers and audiences. Now you must clearly define the model that will allow your team to produce valuable content, products, or services in an accelerated and repeatable way.

Example: Our Team's Phase 2

Early on, we landed a large engagement which allowed us to scale our value hypothesis. This engagement helped us formalize our processes, offerings, and how we engaged with our clients.

Scaling your value will help you home in your marketing model. During this time, you will experience "playing in the grey"—meaning opportunities may arise that you might feel unprepared for. Don't let the discomfort drive you away from pursuing those opportunities. These iterations will move your hypothesis to a well-informed model. For us, that meant formalizing our processes by creating offerings that we could present to a potential new client via a slide presentation as well as performing external research to understand how we could accelerate our growth.

There are two primary ways to generate content for your value-based marketing system. The first is by diversifying your work for clients. The second is by diversifying your team. As your model grows and continues to fulfill your marketing system, think about who you can bring onto your team to provide new perspectives. For example, if your team is currently full of strategists, what would happen if you hired a user experience designer? Or a software engineer? Go back and refer to your team's principles and vision statement to ensure your new hires align to the core mindset of the team, but also ask yourself how you can diversify the skillset on your team that will lead to even greater value you can share with the world.

Phase 3: Scale the Model That Executes and drives the Value (Build It)

Now that you've scaled the value you bring to your audience, it's time to scale the model you clearly defined in Phase 2. By this point, you should have past successes that you can leverage to bring value to new customers. You may be feeling more comfortable with the opportunities coming your way because your offerings solidifying and becoming more foundational. Use that comfort to engage and deliver in dynamic ways.

By scaling your model, you will increase the amount of value you bring to your audience. You can reach bigger audiences, other audiences, and more diverse audiences. Think about the resources your team needs to scale your model. Taking inspiration from the last phase, you might need to grow your team, creating an opportunity to diversify your team's mindset and skillset. You might need more or different technologies or software to scale your model. The best way to figure out what your team needs to scale the model to drive your value-based marketing system is by asking your team members directly. Those who do the work will know what they need to get the work done.

Example: Our Team's Phase 3

We leveraged the formalized processes and offerings we crafted in Phase 2 to scale our model in Phase 3. This is where we began seeing clients approaching us. Our momentum was increasing, and we could offer more types of engagements to leaders and teams throughout our company.

We ensured we had the proper resources to scale our value-based marketing system's model by growing our team. We hired new folks with diverse mindsets and new skills that we didn't previously have. Through proper onboarding to the team's vision and design principles, each new team member was able to bring our brand and value-based marketing system wherever they went and whatever project they were leading.

> **Reflect:** How can you set up a new hire to best represent your team from the start?

Phase 4: Extend Your Model (Defend It)

It is one thing to define your team's brand, and it is another to *embrace* and *execute* the team's brand. Everyone who is a part of the team represents the team's brand.

As you scale your value and model and begin to extend your model, it's important to keep the team's brand in mind to ensure your audience is experiencing a consistent and seamless brand. Included in the team's brand is the voice and visual presence of the team. In our experience, the team's voice has formed naturally as the team continues to evolve and solidify. The team's common voice typically starts from leadership and works its way down (a top-down approach).

When we say the team should have a common voice, we're mainly talking about common phrases and terminology and the "attitude" of voice. This applies to both written and verbal voice. The common voice of a team comes from its shared principles. What has worked best for our team is having one to two team members (this number may vary depending on team size) be the go-to for checking the voice of the team. For example, when a team member writes an article on behalf of the team's publication, that article is reviewed by the team member who is closest to the team's voice.

The team's visual presence connects to branding materials like logos, slide presentation templates, PDF templates, publication layouts, and so on. I suggest having a designer lead and drive the visual presence of your team, and involve your entire team in the process to increase their understanding.

Example: Our Team's Phase 4

This period was the last major evolution in the development of our foundational processes and offerings. With our team's ability to deliver value being proven at a faster rate, and referrals coming in more frequently, our value-based marketing system started running itself. We extended our model by scaling it to other departments and areas within our company. Rather than just supporting teams in the x-department, we scaled our model to bring value to the x-, y-, and z-departments. Because we proved and scaled our value for a specific audience, we were able to easily scale our value-based marketing system's model and, in turn, were able to reach and bring value to more extended audiences.

I picture it as a train. We worked hard in Phases 0 through 3 to get the train running and to control the engine. Now, we can finally add other cars to the locomotive and focus on building those since the engine runs itself. We may sometimes need to refuel or oil a squeaky wheel, but for the most part, we know that the main locomotive engine will keep chugging along as we focus on other parts of the train.

Phase 5: Pursue New Marketing and Value-Driven Milestones, Experiments, and Initiatives (Enable It)

Now you can pursue new milestones and new ways to bring value to your customers. Think outside of the box. How can you be a market disruptor? How can you continue to extend your value but this time to the entire universe? Think big! Dream big! And then turn those thoughts and dreams into reality. Trust that the work you did in Phases 0 through 4 was the right work that allows the core of your value-based marketing system to continue growing on its own.

As we pursue new opportunities, we must communicate our brand up and down, inside and out. This is where our value-based marketing system comes into play. We must promote our brand and content, update and upkeep our brand and market strategy, and have a deep understanding of our future goals and how we want to evolve our marketing strategy.

Creating a brand and marketing strategy is never 'complete.' A marketing strategy requires upkeep; a team member or a subset of the team who is close to the strategy needs to drive it.

Note: Your vision statement should remain the same; if your vision statement needs to change, the essence of your team and your team's purpose has likely changed as well.

At first, the person or subset of the team who will be leading and driving your marketing system will be handling the ideation, content creation, and publication—the end-to-end cycle of a marketing system. Those leaders' goal should be to eventually have a team-wide marketing and brand processes that the entire team understands and contributes to, thus creating a system that, for the most part, operates on its own.

Software and tools exist that may help you maintain your team's marketing system, and I encourage you to research them. Excel or Google Sheets spreadsheets are a good starting point.

The most important task for people leading the team's marketing system is to *teach*, *guide*, and *assist* the rest of the team. Communicate with the rest of the team and be transparent in your marketing system's vision, milestones, goals, and tasks. Ask for assistance from the team and delegate tasks when possible. Eventually, when your value-based marketing system is internally successful, you will end up with a system that runs naturally, and you will then be able to focus on future experiments and new concepts.

Example: Our Team's Phase 5

We began to pursue new milestones by asking ourselves: How can we bring value to even more people, both inside and outside of our company? I was given the opportunity to begin experimenting with ways we could extend our value-based marketing system. Currently, we are focused on extending our digital marketing outreach. We are exploring ways we can publish valuable content to channels like LinkedIn, Medium, and even YouTube through mediums like blog posts, podcasts, one-pagers, and so on. Phase 5 is an ongoing journey of creativity and experimentation. Phase 5 means that we are restlessly assessing new value-creation opportunities and the channels best suited to deliver that value to our audiences. As former GE CMO Beth Comstock says, "Marketing's job is never done. It's about perpetual motion. We must continue to innovate every day."[3]

Key Takeaways

Build Your Value-Based Marketing System

Whether you are starting from scratch or have already been producing content, you must capture the details of your value-based marketing system. Build it with your entire team to ensure cohesion, trust, and pride. Schedule a team-wide meeting, perhaps an offsite, dedicated to building your value-based marketing system together.

Defend Your Value-Based Marketing System

Trust that the value you have defined and promised will positively impact the lives of your audience. Push through the "no's," and believe in your team and vision. Schedule 'meet and greets' with other leaders, teams, and individuals who can benefit from your team's work.

Enable Your Value-Based Marketing System

Never give up on your system. Continuously iterate and evolve it. Push your team's performance in a way that enables you to bring greater and greater value to your audience as your team and value-based marketing system matures. Ask for feedback from your team to understand what is working well and what can be evolved.

CHAPTER 14

Enabling People, Organizations, the World

By Emma Stone

When trees grow together, nutrients and water can be optimally divided among them all so that each tree can grow into the best tree it can be. This is because a tree can be only as strong as the forest that surrounds it.[1]

Trees teach a simple lesson: When we grow, change, and thrive as an ecosystem, everyone wins. When stronger trees get sick over the course of their lives, they depend on their weaker neighbors for support. An individual tree's well-being depends on its community. The forest must continually nourish and enable the growth of others, to enable all to reach new heights.

While this concept is simple, it is not easy. This may explain why it is not well practiced among human organizations. Humans are not nearly as interconnected as trees. Although we are social beings who leverage stories, tools, and technology to foster connection, it is not in our biology to be deeply invested in our neighbor's success. We have the capability to care for our neighbor; we just need the system to do something about it.

This chapter covers the foundations and tools to activate the change-making energy in others so that everyone benefits. Enablement is not a solution; it is a strategic and empathy-driven process. There are four key pillars for putting people, organizations, and the world in a position to achieve their highest potential:

- **Lead with empathy** by understanding and supporting the needs for another's growth and well-being.
- **Adjust your focus** between a zoomed-in forest floor view and a high-level view in the canopy.
- **Cultivate understanding** through a rooted system for continually bringing in new learning and awareness.
- **Drive expansive enablement** by building and finding the right network to continually support.

Lead With Empathy

What does it look like to *lead with empathy* for an individual, a team, an organization, or a world?

- **Individual:** You put the customer first by listening to them intently and innovating on their behalf. Amidst a pandemic, for example, you work rapidly to answer the urgent needs of overwhelmed patients and hospitals by building a new telehealth product. You create the new experience by relying on user personas and journey maps to understand core goals, context, pain points, and needs.
- **Team:** You understand each team member's needs before making a difficult decision on behalf of the entire team (particularly when that decision counters standard practice). During a pandemic or crisis, you allot thirty minutes in the middle of a workday for the team to meditate or set up flexible working hours so individuals can process and effectively manage their situations.
- **Organization:** You take the initiative to learn and connect with a group of people who are not apparently impacted by your day-to-day business actions, but could be, and *ought to be*. You create an enterprise-wide mindfulness initiative to offer evidence-based training and regular meditation sessions that improve employee well-being and compassion.
- **World:** You recognize that there is power in your seemingly small actions to cause aggregational disruption in the world,

for good and for bad. You calculate your team's carbon
footprint based on the number of plane flights they've taken
and reconcile it by planting enough trees to go carbon-positive.

We believe that leading with empathy is about stepping away from
the immediate action asked of you—the solution, the decision, the business objective—and stepping into *who* that action impacts—the individual, the organization, the world.

Adjust Your Focus

People are at the center of everything we do. Whether we are zooming in
on an individual, out on organizational dynamics, or applying a wide lens
to view people in the context of their world, our goal is to have an **impact
mindset.** In doing so, the impact we create is through the enablement of
others. There is a causal impact of making space for others.

The way we see people through different lenses will affect our strategy
for enablement. There are two key vantage points: a zoomed-in approach
and a zoomed-out approach. This follows the innate pattern of human
cognition. There is a common oversimplification of how the right- and
left-brain work. Many consider the left brain as logistical and the right
brain as creative. According to psychiatrist Iain McGilchrist, it is more
complicated. Each side of the brain does everything the other does, but
they perceive the world slightly differently. The left side focuses on the
details, while the right side focuses on the bigger picture. The left side is
needed to complete targeted tasks, and the right side is needed for a broad
and sustained understanding of why the tasks matter. They produce two
different yet essential views of reality.[2]

Zooming In (left brain)

A zoomed-in approach is applying a targeted focus to make salient details
clear. Without narrowing in on a problem, you will miss important details
and make unfounded decisions. Reading a research paper will not deliver
the rawness of human motivation and pain, but an interaction will. For a
problem's root cause to resonate, you must see it firsthand.

Zooming Out (right brain)

A zoomed-out approach provides a full map of the problem and the implications that come with it. You can make big-picture decisions from this vantage. A holistic view of a problem requires that you look for themes or commonalities and ask why something keeps happening. Most high-complexity, systems-level problems have long-term implications that need to be respected and considered.

As we understand a problem from both vantage points, we must lead with empathy. In your next project or initiative, try defining the problem from both lenses. Take note of what is gained and lost in each view, then determine how you go about addressing both in your proposed resolution.

Effectively oscillating between the views will take your team to the next level of human-organizational-world impact. For example, successful teams consider and connect to their consumers with an empathetic lens by understanding their goals, motivations, and needs. Better teams will do this while operating with a strong awareness and respect for their organization's needs and goals. This is often where the action-oriented empathy stops on an enterprise team. Most teams rarely look beyond the needs of their consumers and colleagues. A small number of top teams will consider how world events influence and inspire their business agenda. Even fewer teams will deliberately add world events to their agenda and act on them at a global scale.

High-performing enterprise teams do all the above.

A World Focus

Every team needs to make a conscious choice around how they see and acknowledge the rest of the world while performing their day job. From a neurobiological perspective, one's environment has an overwhelming influence on one's thoughts and behaviors. This means nothing and no one can be understood in a vacuum. When we step into our "work lives," it is impossible to fully detach from our personal lives.

We are constantly aware and influenced by the world pressing up against the office walls and the virtual meeting's dial tones. Humans are capable of temporarily compartmentalizing, but the human experience is continuous, and the brain does not discriminate based on whether an experience occurred in a work or nonwork setting. The frustration from the morning's traffic may keep you on edge all morning, an impending call about a diagnosis may make you anxious all afternoon, and your involvement in civil protests may redirect your focus from tomorrow's quarterly presentation. There is no distinct separation of world events and workplace events, any socially constructed barrier between the two may restrict your team's progress. There may be more synergy between the social justice movement and your business agenda than you realize.

> **Reflect:** Next time you review the day's news and current events, look to find the thread and relevance to your work. How might it impact your employee experience, strategy, and measure of success?

Your *weltanschauung* is the way you see the world from your current position based on the knowledge you have and the experiences that have shaped you. High-performing teams strive to continuously feed and inform their weltanschauung by stepping outside their fishbowl, understanding their role, and staying one step ahead.

> There are these two young fish swimming along, and they happen to meet an older fish swimming the other way, who nods at them and says "Morning boys. How's the water?" And the two young fish swim on for a bit, and then eventually one of them looks over at the other and goes "What the hell is water?"[3]
>
> —David Foster Wallace

Worldly Empathy Sets High-Performing Enterprise Teams Apart

Worldly empathy is taking on the responsibility to learn about problems and people beyond your product, team, and company walls. It is actively listening to, educating on, and engaging with world topics with the intention to make positive changes in new spaces. This is how we can recognize the water we swim in. The outcome of world empathy is unprecedented global impact, driven by understanding and expansive enablement, as seen in Figure 14.1. It is not always clear how we can best serve or improve a

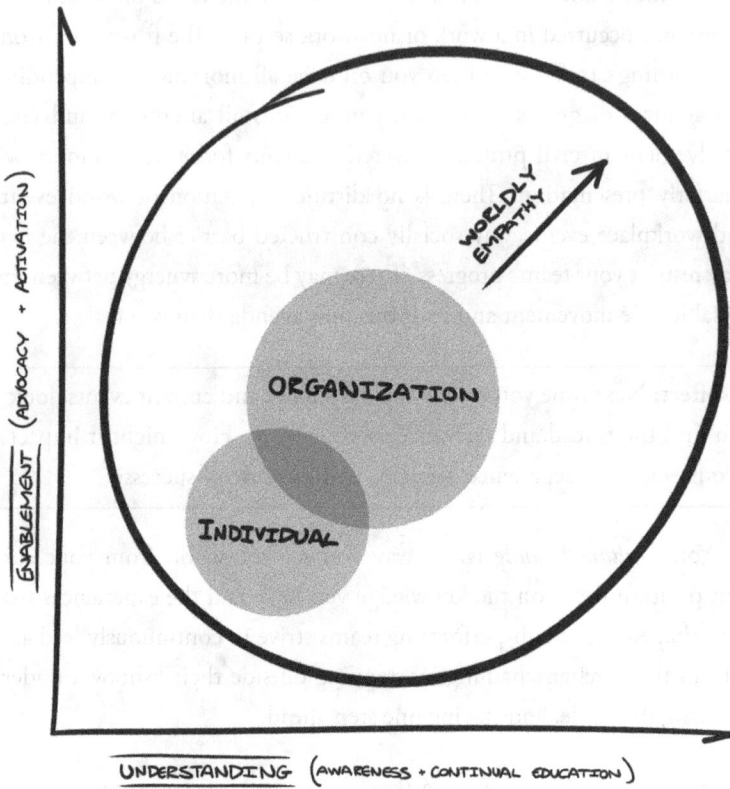

Figure 14.1 Increasing world empathy

When high-performing enterprise teams go beyond themselves and their organization to cultivate worldly empathy through their widespread understanding and enablement, they create unprecedented global impact. In this figure, circle size represents impact potential.

situation beyond our immediate context. The high-performing team will research, raise awareness, tap into their toolkit, or create new tools and processes to impact their world.

Cultivate Understanding

Worldly Awareness

Impact cannot be made without profound awareness. The first step to embody worldly empathy is to foster worldly awareness in the workplace. The only way teams will create new and ever-growing impact in the world is by increasing their appetite and channels to become more aware.

We believe that conversations about the world "outside of work" should be brought inside of work when it has immediate implications for individual well-being or global action.

> **Reflect:** Have you ever been in a professional setting in which your colleagues avoided a recent major world event?

Our team relies on four foundations to recognize personal boundaries, personhood, and our connection to events outside our immediate context:

1. Psychological safety
2. Topical ideation
3. Consistent channels to cultivate our awareness
4. Active listening

Psychological Safety

Through worldly awareness, we are able to recognize our team's position in the context of our broader community and shared humanity. For this to happen successfully, there needs to be an environment of psychological safety and trust on the team. Members of the team must know that topics outside current projects and business priorities will be received with interest and openness. Importantly, it is safe for every voice, no matter the background, lived experience, years of experience, or job title.

As a personal example, I was empowered to lead 18 more "senior" members through a workshop on accessibility with less than a year of experience on the team. Not only was I given the platform to share my voice and perspective, but the team members were active listeners, enabling me so that I could enable them. Think about your current team—who might need improved psychological safety to come forward with an idea or topic? Consider the structural inequities that often silence some voices more than others: race, gender, sexual orientation, disability, and age.

Topical Ideation

High-performing teams hold high expectations for their team members. That is why everyone is afforded an equal opportunity and platform to raise issues or worldly awareness. In exchange for this platform and active engagement from the team, there is a shared trust that any new topic or training being brought to the collective has important implications for the team and our work. In other words, while the topic or global issue may not overtly relate to ongoing work, it likely suggests a new way of thinking, a new approach, or a new opportunity to make significant impact through our work.

High-Performing Teams Seek the Deep-Rooted Meaning in a Topical Issue to Create Massive Impact in New Spaces

By discussing the ideas that emerge from stories of people or world events, we deepen our understanding of human behavior and the implications of

Table 14.1 Turning ideas into actions

Person/group	Event	Idea	Example actions
Virtual workforce	COVID-19 sending people to work from home indefinitely	How might we relieve some of the stress caused by the need to adapt to new environments and routines that may keep individuals from being able to bring their full selves to work?	• Provide team-wide mental health day and regular company wide mindfulness sessions. • Adopt flexible working hours.
Local physicians and medical clinics	COVID-19 putting our frontline workers at high risk	How might we use our own skills and resources to serve and reduce risk for frontline workers?	• Host an atomic hour to help clinics strategically redesign their clinical spaces and digital health models.
George Floyd	Police brutality, Nationwide Black Lives Matter protests	How might we recognize and address characteristics of white supremacy in our own organizational processes and culture?	• Change our hiring practices and recruitment channels to promote a more diverse workforce on our team and across the organization. • Host equity pauses, including Notice and Reflect practices in design methods.

the event. This topical ideation is how we find solutions to help the world, rather than contributing to the noise, as displayed in Table 14.1.

Consistent Channels

Worldly awareness requires that the right channels are in place to allow these ideas and conversations to enter the workplace in meaningful ways. The right channels can be recurring messages, team rituals for surfacing topics, or an email to a small group of teammates. Our team designates Thursday standups for a teachable takeover at least once a month where any teammate can prepare and present a topic for 30 to 60 minutes. Some topics include mindfulness, unconscious bias, cultural anthropology, pace layering, diverse networking, Black Lives Matter movement, climate change, disability inclusion, inclusive design, and physician burnout. We have more informal channels like our messaging channel called "World." We post learnings, articles, and perspectives on things happening outside company walls. This content often informs the deep discussion in team trainings or Thursday standups. Other times, it is used to extend empathy by recognizing a team member in their world context:

> [MS Teams Message, Nov 10th, 12:09 PM] Fusion Team—Just a quick PSA. I am generally not fear driven, but believe in being thoughtful. *I personally believe* no matter which candidate is elected to office we will have some period of unrest. What form that will take no one can predict. I would say put some thought to it for you and your family and what that might mean. I care about you and your personal safety, that's the Why behind the message.

Active Listening

The fourth foundation for channeling awareness is **active listening**. Active listening is essential for deep awareness and understanding another's experience. Different from simply "listening," *active* listening involves a conscious effort to understand the complete message and context of what is being said. On an individual level, it means having undivided attention for the speaker, and using the subtleties of body language and voice to interpret another's true meaning and demonstrate your genuine engagement. On the worldly level, it means paying attention to different media sources and noticing shifts in trends that draw meaning and provoke thought. High-performing teams think of themselves as world research analysts. The same way that a market researcher gathers data and listens to the market, we gather insight and listen to societal needs.

An experiment worth trying: identify one person or team who you want to better understand. Set up a meeting and test your active listening skills by allowing room for long pauses and time for open-ended questions.

Worldly awareness is a combination of internal and external awareness. To respond effectively to a broader problem, we must recognize our individual position and our team's position in relation to that problem. Once we understand our own strengths and shortcomings, we can begin to understand our role in enabling others.

Continuous Education

Allyship is never declared, it is always bestowed
                                             —Senator Sarah McBride

To be action-oriented and world-changing, awareness must be fed by continuous education and engagement. Once a topical idea is channeled into the high-performing team, everyone goes hunting for blind spots and collaborates to build each other's expertise.

R   **L**

Place a hand over your right eye. Now, focus on the "**L**" above with your left eye. Start moving toward or away from the screen until you find a position where you cannot see the "**R**" in your periphery. If successful, you have found your visual blind spot. The effect is interesting for two reasons. First, it suggests we can become aware of our blind spots when we change our perspective. Second, it indicates that we can have access to complete information but fail to perceive it holistically.

Changed perspective starts with education and education starts with the individual. We do not rely on the teammate or source of new information to drive our understanding. Although I was initially perceived as the "expert" on accessibility because I conducted the training, everyone understood they could become an ally. Each team member branched out and brought new insight from different parts of our world to strengthen the team's overall understanding. Educating oneself on systemic or societal issues takes work and commitment. It takes work because it often requires that we unlearn and relearn. As mentioned in Chapter 3, "Inclusion and Diversity," we must not only recognize that our perception of an issue is inaccurate or incomplete; we must challenge our personal cognitive biases that have been so strongly wired in our brains.

Ways to educate oneself on a topical issue may include the following:

1. **Read:** books, research articles, news stories, company resources
2. **Observe:** documentaries, user testing, colleagues
3. **Listen:** podcasts, feedback, company conversations
4. **Engage:** volunteer, follow influencers, extend your network, take a course

At first glance, nothing in this "ROLE" toolkit is groundbreaking; most of us know how to intake new information. However, we rarely use these resources to actively grapple with a new topic. It is in our neurobiology to default to what we know within our routine, content intake, and social groups. To branch out effectively, teams need to embrace ROLE and a **fear no topic mindset**. By leaving no topic unturned, we maximize the chance of a radical and inspired solution. Even if it doesn't lead to a solution, it is our responsibility to grow through the discomfort. When was the last time you were uncomfortably learning? Identify one topical issue that you know little about—climate change, artificial intelligence, overpopulation, extreme poverty, food security, water pollution, maternal health, urbanization, LGBTQ+ discrimination, international law—anything happening at a national or global scale. Once you choose a topic for which you have surface-level knowledge, it is time to go a few levels below the surface; four levels deeper to be exact. Explore the topic by going through the four different channels in the ROLE model.

Although education starts with the individual, it is not an independent endeavor. Inviting the whole team into your educational journey will maximize knowledge sharing and impact. Essential qualities for this collective journey are humility and vulnerability. Humility comes from admitting you do not know as much as you should. Vulnerability comes from exposing that ignorance to the rest of the team. It is difficult to reshape our own views, and it is just as difficult to shape an environment in which those views can be freely shared. The goal for a vulnerable learning process can be nurtured on the team.

Methods for creating an environment for engaged learning:

- Embrace a Radical Candor4 feedback model to help teammates with blind spots.
- Create an open forum to submit questions after an educational training or event.
- Feed new learnings directly into the team Blueprint (see Chapter 8, "Value Blueprinting").
- Hold small group discussions on heavy topics before bringing to the wider group.

As a high-performing enterprise team, limiting learning to self-discovery and personal experience is not an option. Not only do we extend beyond the individual but we also have a responsibility to reach outside our team circle and bring in new insight. We regularly invite senior leaders to speak, most of whom we have never met or worked alongside.

In these 30-minute *Meet and Greet* sessions, we follow a clear pattern:

- The guest leader introduces their role, personal why, and ongoing work (more on "personal why" in Chapter 1, "Purpose, Passion, People").
- Our team learns something new about the organization to keep in the collective knowledge bank.
- Our team asks a series of questions to understand how we are uniquely positioned to help this leader in their role—in other words, we clarify and identify the "Jobs to be Done."[5]

- Our team's collective understanding of an industry-wide or global issue is enhanced.
- Our team's call to action is reinforced.

Meet and Greets are not a networking tactic; they are an enabler. The team leaves with a more holistic understanding of the problem, while leaders leave knowing a full team of people is dedicated to collaboratively address that problem.

In addition to bringing people in to discuss complex problems, engagement also means getting the team outside their comfort zone. For example, the full team should be volunteering in the community, attending webinars, panels, and discussion groups, or following new leaders and influencers on social media. One of the best ways to learn is through direct engagement. When it comes to worldly empathy, this often means engaging with groups of people who are disproportionately affected by the world events and the systemic issues we are trying to address. Pause for a moment and reflect: Does the makeup of your team fully and authentically reflect the customers, consumers, and stakeholders you aim to serve? If not, do you regularly address the gaps by bringing in external insight or feedback? Human-centered design is only "human" if it recognizes that there is not one universal human experience. Therefore, we need to be co-developing, co-designing, and working alongside people with those diverse lived experiences.

When *Team* Becomes *Teacher* . . . but Stays the *Student*

As the team becomes more educated and engaged, the work is far from done. The team moves quickly. The high-performing team learns and engages best when they take the initiative to teach and engage others shortly after their own learning. Because the high-performing team is often ahead of the curve, they have a responsibility to bring others up to speed. They do not claim to have all the answers, instead recognizing the need to spread ideas and get to work quickly. We operate with the understanding that the greatest barriers to enablement and transformative change are self-imposed: lack of knowledge and fear surrounding the issue. We need to know enough to be thoughtful and strategic, but we cannot let the fear of not knowing *everything* keep us from doing *anything* at all.

The informed enterprise team strives to bring clarity to others, and we strive to make learning and engagement as easy as possible, to rapidly build momentum and energy. That is why we create materials and tools to spread awareness, in addition to connecting others with the resources that forged our own learning. This may take the form of tangible resources like Medium articles, one-pager infographics, and how-to resource decks to designed environments like virtual trainings and spaces for reflection. That said, it is more than simply surfacing and sharing documents. If that were the case, LinkedIn would have resolved climate change and world hunger by now. The best way to engage new learning, and the only way to motivate real behavior change is to integrate the problem with narrative and storytelling. The story makes a problem relational, rather than transactional, which makes change transformational, rather than provisional.

This effort is less about giving teams, groups, and organizations outside our team the "answer," and more about enabling them to arrive at their own answer. We do everything in our power to clear the weeds and sow the first seeds, but it is not our garden alone. It is up to others to respond with their own expertise and nurture new breakthroughs.

Drive Expansive Enablement: Enablement Is Not a Heroic Act, but a Humbling One

For worldly empathy to create a massive impact, it must drive expansive enablement. High-performing teams have diverse abilities, and they also look beyond themselves to cultivate the expansive enablement of other people. Through their worldly awareness and extensive education and engagement, high-performing teams seek to elevate the knowledge, experience, and performance of others. We use our unique position and influence to enable as many people as possible. We strive to be radically self-aware, which means deeply connecting to how we can make an impact and direct action or initiate change. This also means understanding where we would be *unhelpful*. It's easy to fall into egocentricity, where we overemphasize our role in events we seek to explain. Overemphasizing can contribute to the fundamental attribution error, where we ascribe more importance and positive intent to our actions than to others. Becoming an enabler is recognition that you can make a process easier, but you cannot carry it out fully on someone or some entity's behalf. Inherent in this is the recognition that you can just as easily be an inhibitor if you're not careful.

In our view, enablement is not a handout; it is an activation. We believe that society has failed when someone is unable to effectively participate in the world. Enablement focuses on changing society or the environment, rather than changing the person or group of people so that others can reach their potential.

Advocacy

Advocacy is the first part of ensuring others can achieve their potential. Amidst the ongoing awareness and education, high-performing teams will advocate for those who have been systematically under-resourced and marginalized. They embrace the idea that if we are not actively dismantling the system, then we are endorsing it.

Advocacy is not limited to participating in rallies, protests, and fundraising events. Decisions and actions we take as business leaders, technologists, and innovators make a difference. This may take the form of explicit vocal support or defense on behalf of another. For example, providing feedback to a colleague that their presentation and specific font choices fail to consider those with visual disabilities. It may also take a more implicit form in the way we approach our work. For instance, sending the presentation deck before the start of a meeting so that those with visual impairments can review them ahead of time and follow along.

High-performing enterprise teams act as the example without being the protagonist. The protagonist is the person or group for whom we are advocating. Rather than own or share the story, the team's purpose is to bring awareness to the story.

We create the opportunity for others to share their story when we check our own biases and open our doors. Sometimes, that means embracing an **equity pause** to reflect on our own language, ideas, and biases; sometimes it means actively deconstructing and redesigning practices that perpetuate a harmful culture. Breaking down the barrier to entry and opening an equitable, safe space for others to excel is the second part of enablement. These actions are built on the strongly held belief that what keeps many from reaching their fullest potential are the barriers and limitations society puts on them.

> **Equity Pause:** Strategic equity pauses to stop the clock and reflect on our language, ideas, and hunches in the context of a discourse of transformation. Without this moment to think, our brains default to the familiar and the known, making a repeat of past practice likely. Incorporating these discourse checks and pauses after each stage ensures that our ideas remain on the path of achieving equity.[6]

Once the high-performing enterprise team has helped create a space, they are obligated to accelerate and nurture the growth. There are two types of supporters: *carpenters* and *gardeners*. We strive to be gardeners. By providing the nutrients rather than the blueprint, others will embody their authentic selves and rise to their fullest potential. We enable growth by pushing each other and those whom we advocate for to the edge of their comfort level. People in this learn and develop the fastest. It may manifest as a challenging project for an individual, a new partner for the organization, or a provocative published work for the world. Enablement is not *the* solution, but rather the crucial trigger for someone else to arrive at a solution.

Activation

The final step to enablement is activating autonomy. Autonomy is the greatest intrinsic motivation for becoming a top performer and world changer. Once autonomy is activated and realized, people and organizations become unstoppable. For the high-performing enterprise team, the only job left is to orient and get out of the way.

By branching out to enable another's autonomy, we allow every individual to contribute and support the overall ecosystem in a way that we, alone, could not. When this happens, the entire forest grows stronger.

"The contributions of forests to the well-being of humankind are extraordinarily vast and far-reaching."[7]

Key Takeaways

Adjust Your Lens

Seeing people through different lenses will affect our strategy for enablement. There are two key vantage points: a zoomed-in approach and a zoomed-out approach. We must continue to lead with empathy as we understand a problem from both vantage points. In your next project or initiative, try defining the problem from both lenses. Take note of what is gained and lost in each view, then determine how you go about addressing both in your proposed resolution.

Cultivate Worldly Empathy Through Awareness and Education

World empathy is actively listening to, educating on, and engaging with world topics with the intention to make positive changes in new spaces. Teams need to embrace consistent worldly channels, a fear no topic mindset, and a vulnerable, engaged learning style to successfully cultivate worldly empathy. Next time you review the day's news and current events, look to find the thread and relevance to your work. How might it impact your employee experience, strategy, and measure of success?

Set the Stage for Expansive Enablement

The high-performing team learns and engages best when they take the initiative to teach and engage others shortly after their own learning. Because the high-performing team is often ahead of the curve, they have a responsibility to bring others up to speed. They use their unique position and influence to enable as many people as possible, no matter who they are and no matter what their needs are. Build the foundation for a learning system by creating space for each teammate to teach others. Host discussions, invite outside perspectives, and make room for story.

The End Goal Is Activation and Autonomy

Massive impact is created by activating someone else's potential for impact, creating an exponential and radiant effect. Identify one barrier a teammate or customer is confronting that is stalling them. Then, do everything in your power to remove that obstacle. Once autonomy is activated and realized, people and organizations become unstoppable.

CHAPTER 15

Creating Conscious Connections

By Julie Williams

Imagine that you can travel through time. Take yourself back to the start of your day. Think about where you have gone and who you have seen. Maybe you had breakfast with your family, spoke with a friend on the phone, or waved to a neighbor. Maybe you ordered coffee from your favorite barista, chatted with your colleague, or attended an exercise class. We experience countless interactions every single day. They can be big or small, short or long, positive or negative. They all impact us. And we impact the people around us. We all exist as contributors to our complicated ecosystems. Our interactions are connected, ongoing, and lasting.

What Role Do We Want to Play?

We Have an Obligation to Make Our World a Better Place

Understanding that our actions have deep impact means we need to make a conscious choice. What role do we want to play? Fusion has committed to embracing positivity and optimism, practicing kindness and servant leadership, and supporting each other in achieving success. This is true both within our team and within our broader ecosystem. Our commitment, combined with our team's passions, skills, and relationships, has increased our entire ecosystem's access to knowledge, camaraderie, and support, driving all of us forward in our shared goal of improving healthcare for all.

In this chapter, we will explore the role your team plays within its ecosystem, with a specific lens on skills-based volunteering. We will dive deep into the Conscious Connections Model and discover how impact can be amplified when your team has:

- Deep knowledge of the **needs and resources** within your **communities**.
- An understanding of **passions and skills**.
- Strong **relationships** with nonprofits committed to creating impact.
- **Ecosystems** that support meaningful change.

Teams that approach giving with empathy and combine the powers above enable organizations that are changing the world.

Giving With Empathy

Empathy Is at the Core of Impact

Practicing empathy, as emphasized in Chapter 14, "Enabling People, Organizations, the World," places us in the minds of those involved in the giving ecosystem and enables us to understand each stakeholder's wants, needs, and goals. This leads to alignment in our desired outcomes and ensures that our servant leadership and volunteering is relevant and meaningful to nonprofits and the individuals whom they serve.

Empathy for Nonprofit Partners

"I Am Working to Put Myself Out of a Job."

Ask any nonprofit employee why they chose their field of work. You will likely hear the individual wants to make change in their community. They may feel a connection to a particular population or cause or be driven by a desire to have a purposeful life. No matter whom you ask or the specifics of the response, there is always one common thread that ties their *why* together: Nonprofit employees care deeply about their work. As I am sure you have experienced, caring deeply is hard. It takes time, effort, and brainpower. In the nonprofit sector, it also comes with a feeling of obligation—the need to constantly do better for the people you serve, your community, and the world. Depending on the day, the sense of obligation can lead to high levels of stress or great joys.

Caring deeply is a huge investment. Just like for-profit companies, nonprofit leaders have knowledge and expertise in their field and a strong connection to the people that they serve. They understand the external factors that impact access to resources and the way they work. They strategize and have a vision of how to push forward. Nonprofit leaders have great skills and know what needs to be done for their organizations to be successful.

Scarce resources (funds, staffing, expertise, and time) can slow progress. This is where volunteers—your team!—come in. Volunteers have the potential to be a great asset, providing support and augmenting limited resources. They also can pose a great challenge. Nonprofits have a big ask for skills-based volunteers: to give their time and skills with no payment in return. If the volunteer is not the right fit or misunderstands the nonprofit's needs and level of commitment, volunteer turnover occurs. Projects slow or are stopped in their tracks—the total opposite of conscious connectivity and impact.

I have learned the importance of having empathy for nonprofits first-hand. A community theater that I historically volunteered for reached out to me, asking me to join the committee that would determine the plays for the theater's upcoming season. This was a time-consuming job that included researching plays and musicals, reading hundreds of pages, determining season fit, and writing recommendations. I said "yes," not to support the theater, but to please the friend who contacted me. I did not take the nonprofit's needs into account. I did not feel a connection to the specific area where help was requested, and I did not commit to the relationship with the theater itself.

My lack of empathy and time got the best of me. I selfishly put off my commitments. I started to miss deadlines, and, after some deep reflection, I went back to the committee with my apologies and stepped down from my role, knowing that I was not going to complete my task.

This was a big setback for the theater, who put their timeline on hold to include my thoughts, which never came. My incomplete work then needed to be shifted to other committee members, who had already dutifully completed their tasks. This was an embarrassing moment for me— to say the least—but a mistake I will never make again, and a mistake you can now avoid as well.

It is our job, as volunteers, to empathize with the nonprofits in our ecosystem so we can:

- Understand the burdens and wins that come with caring deeply.
- Respect nonprofit leaders' expertise.
- Give where help is needed.
- Commit to the nonprofit relationship.

Empathy for Ourselves

Understand Your Why to Commit to Good

Volunteering requires empathy for ourselves. As touched on, the job of "volunteer" is not always an easy one. It requires time, skills, and relationship building. Depending on the needs of the nonprofit and the project or role your team takes on, volunteering can be a big commitment.

Think back to Chapter 1, "Purpose, Passion, People," and find your personal *why*. Just as your *why* should be integrated into work and goals, it should also be integrated into volunteering. Knowing your *why*—and specifically in this instance, your team's *why*—is an important step toward impact. It allows your team to answer a critical question: Why do we want to get involved? Exploring your team's *why* will uncover what motivates team members to volunteer and give. You may discover that your team has a deeply ingrained *why* that drives support toward a specific community, nonprofit, or cause. You may find that your team is motivated by building relationships and expanding its ecosystem. Or that teammates feel empowered when using skills for good. Without this *why*, your team may fall into the trap of compulsory volunteering because it feels expected. It is important to make sure your team's *why* is strong enough to make a commitment and follow through, even when that commitment becomes challenging.

Logistics also come into play. Our availability ebbs and flows. After deciding to volunteer, do a quick calendar check to confirm that the team has the time to give without the new commitment feeling like a burden. All team members will be grateful for the capacity check before diving into a new project, even if the project is a rewarding one!

> **Reflect:** Why do we want to get involved? Are we really able to make a commitment to this?

The Conscious Connections Model

Flexing our empathy muscle has brought us to the point of commitment. The Conscious Connections Model (Figure 15.1) bridges our *why* to our *how*. It asks us to:

- Understand **community needs**.
- Celebrate team **passions**.
- Align with **organizations** in our ecosystems.
- Reflect on team **skills**.

When these four dimensions—community needs, passions, organizations, and skills—converge, we get a clear picture of *how* teams can create impact and provide value to nonprofit partners.

Figure 15.1 Conscious Connections model

Model dimensions converge to create impact.

Dimension 1: Community Needs

Communities Drive Our Purpose

Teams and their members belong to multiple communities and our communities take many forms. They are built around shared locations, beliefs, relationships, experiences, and identities. Some communities are chosen for us, while others are self-selected. Regardless of how we come to belong, communities help us feel accepted and included. They shape our experiences and give us purpose and a sense of self. They enable deep connections and lasting relationships.

Communities also experience needs, big and small, that cause discomfort or pain and drive our desire to make change and take action. It is essential that we reflect on these needs to understand the root causes and effects on our communities. Determining the nature and urgency of each need directs us to *where* we can help and drive positive change.

Think broadly as your team reflects on community needs. Many times, our brains jump to economic needs, like hunger or housing. While extremely important, we must consider the needs that extend beyond economics. In doing so, we uncover challenges around land preservation, arts and culture, education, and social justice (to name a few).

Reflect: To what communities does our team belong? What needs exist within these communities? Why do these needs exist?

Answering these questions unveils team and team member ecosystems, and where these ecosystems overlap. It also identifies which needs are most prevalent within your team's communities. Remember to document as you build out your list of needs. We will revisit this list as our model dimensions converge.

Dimension 2: Passions

Passions Accelerate Impact

Passions represent what we care deeply about. They are boundless and make us relatable, interesting, and unique. Passions drive and motivate us. They also dictate where we spend our most precious resource—our time. As volunteering takes a great deal of time, it is important to embrace and align team passions when deciding where to give. This allows teams to commit with ease and eliminates feelings of burden.

We can think about passions in two ways, from a *giving lens* and from a *personal lens*. When approaching from a lens of giving, our passions will be focused and tailored. Our list might include climate change, social justice, or STEM education. When looking from a personal lens, we think about our passions generally. Our list might include hiking, cooking, watching movies, or spending time with family. Like our passions in giving, our personal passions can be translated into impact. For example, I have a personal passion for bringing friends and family together and for creating space for people to build meaningful relationships. This passion transformed into a volunteer role, through which I brought together a diverse group of youth and coached them through learning about and participating in local philanthropy.

> **Reflect** from a personal lens and a giving lens to guide your team's giving journey. The key questions to ask your team are: What are our team's deepest passions? What causes do we care about?

As your team builds its list, it will uncover the passions of the team itself and of its team members. This practice builds interest, excitement, and engagement and is a big accelerator for two reasons:

1. Teams can identify overlaps in passions across all members and together support a single organization or project.
2. Teams can build subgroups of individuals with similar interests and share passions across multiple projects.

Both options establish strong connections and commitment to organizations and allow teams to address projects and needs that they care about deeply.

Tying Together Passions and Needs: Align Passions and Needs to Uncover Your *What*

You may have noticed as you documented passions that some passions overlap with the community needs identified by your team. This is an important realization. Areas of overlap point you to the causes that your team wants to support. Giving where teammates are passionate will ease commitment and bring fulfillment while creating impact.

> **Reflect:** Take a moment to review identified community needs and passions.

Formally document the overlap, which will tell you *what* cause your team wants to support. This *what* will be a key input as we move into the third dimension of our model. When completing this process, be creative in your pairing; some overlap might not be immediately obvious. For example, once when volunteering with friends, we together identified a need for hunger relief and a shared passion for being outdoors. This passion for the outdoors led us to plant thousands of vegetables at a community farm that harvests produce for local food pantries.

Dimension 3: Organizations

Organizational Alignment Ensures Shared Passions and Goals

Now that we have determined *what* we want to support, we need to consider the resources that exist in our communities—the nonprofits themselves. Each nonprofit has a mission outlining what they do and why they do it. These missions drive nonprofits forward and act as the anchor for all strategic decisions. Aligning your team's *what* to a partner organization's mission determines our *where* and ensures that everyone is working toward a common goal.

We are now going to explore organizations from the lens of our *where*, looking specifically for nonprofits that align with team passions and support identified needs. Conduct an online search for nonprofits that are addressing the needs that your team wants to support. You will gain access to relevant organizations through this search. Take a quick

Table 15.1 Organization exploration grid

Organization	Mission and Vision	Programs and Services	Population Served	Organization Impact	Volunteer Opportunities	Contact Information
Organization 1						
Organization 2						

tour of each website, being sure to stop and document the mission and vision, programs and services, population served, organization impact, volunteer opportunities, and contact information for each organization, as illustrated in Table 15.1.

The team can also explore the following sources to gather additional insightful information:

- Social media—understand current happenings
- News articles—learn about recent efforts or accomplishments
- CharityNavigator.org—review nonprofit impact ratings
- Guidestar.org—gather information on organization financials (Form 990s)
- GreatNonprofits.org—view nonprofit reviews from stakeholders

While research will get your team far, it will not give a full picture of a nonprofit's work. As you near the end of your web search, it is time to pick up the phone. Nonprofit employees love talking about their work and will likely be more than happy to chat. For initial conversations, call those working in development (the nonprofit term for fundraising) and those working in programs. Keep questions open-ended to gather as much information as possible. Consider asking about the organization itself, needs being addressed, programs and services offered, funding sources, successes and challenges, and future goals. Don't forget to ask if the nonprofit is looking for any project or volunteer support!

In addition to fueling your team's passions, detailed in Dimension 1, this exploratory process will provide a list of organizations that alleviate the needs your team cares about and will help you understand the projects that organizations are looking to tackle.

Dimension 4: Skills

Skills Are a Catalyst for Change

The final piece to align is our fourth dimension: skills. Skills highlight our talents and expertise. They can be hard or soft and can be applied to many situations, both at work and in life. Just as with passions, skills are unbounded and varied. They help us solve problems, make decisions, and accomplish goals. Everyone has a unique set of skills that brings value to a community. Celebrating diversity of skill allows us to bring together individuals who complement and challenge each other to grow. It also enables teams to practice servant leadership, using skills for good. When identifying core skills within our teams, we want to consider *work skills* (e.g., strategic or creative thinking, graphic design programing, process management), *personal skills* (e.g., painting, playing an instrument, gardening, home organization), and skills that bridge both work and personal spheres (e.g., prioritization, organization, communication, relationship building).

All skills can provide great value, depending on nonprofit needs. You may find a teammate's skills in home organization are just as important as their skills in graphic design. Last, don't ignore the skills that teammates are working to develop. Supporting a nonprofit through learning-by-doing is a great way to simultaneously give and grow your team.

Reflect: What are our team's skills (professional and personal)? What skills do we want to develop? Be sure to document your answers!

The resulting list provides insight into what your team can offer the nonprofits impacting your communities. Through this exercise, your team will gain a sense of its overall skills as well as each team member's skills, and how individual's core skills complement each other to achieve success. Bringing these varied skills and viewpoints to a nonprofit—especially to an area where a nonprofit is experiencing a gap—can have a big impact on an organization, project, and community.

Tying Together Opportunities and Skills

We have reached the last step in our model—aligning nonprofit projects with skills to find our *how*. Revisit the nonprofits identified through your research and the projects that are available. Identify the skills that these projects may require and where your team's skills overlap. The projects that overlap are the projects to pursue. These are the projects that support the nonprofits that share your team's passions and need your skills. These are the projects the team can meaningfully support and accelerate forward.

Create Massive Value

Value Comes in Many Forms

Now that we have our *how*, there is one remaining question: What types of support might nonprofits be looking for? Nonprofits face many varied challenges. Some are similar to those we experience in the for-profit world, including strategic planning, team building, impact measurement, and branding. Others are more specific to the field, like creating fundraising campaigns, meaningfully engaging donors, providing value to volunteers, and managing grants.

Nonprofits are constantly trying to balance goals and resources. They are endlessly creative and resourceful in maintaining this balance and require varied supports as different challenges arise. These supports generally take the form of short-term problem solving or long-term relationships. Note that short-term and long-term references project length. When determining your team's ability to give (think back to empathy for yourself!), outline how much time teammates are willing and able to spend. This could be 10 hours a week or 10 hours a month—whatever amount of time will allow your team to make a meaningful commitment to the organization you are supporting without that commitment being a burden.

Short-Term Problem Solving

Typically, with short-term problem solving, a nonprofit has identified a specific need within the organization and requires targeted support. Short-term engagements are generally project-based. They have a clear scope of work and an understood start and end date. Often, the organization will be looking for skills that they don't have access to in-house. These engagements are a great way to bring impact efficiently and effectively to an organization.

Long-Term Relationships

Nonprofits have long-term, ongoing needs as well. These can take the form of multimonth projects like completing a full re-brand, implementing new technology, or scouting for a location move. They can also take a similar form to a job. Many nonprofits "employ" volunteers to own key tasks, like grant writing or program development. The job most commonly associated with nonprofits is board membership. In this role, trustees take on the duty of oversight and fiscal responsibility for an organization—a role not to be taken lightly!

Long-term engagements require a great deal of expertise that non-profits rely on and value. They also require adaptability and patience, as timelines and scopes may change as work progresses and relationships adapt. Teams who commit to the relationship and dedicate their skills to these engagements drive consistent, positive change and reap great personal reward.

Fusion's commitment to social impact led us to a long-term engagement with a local community center. The center initially reached out to participate in a Fusion Atomic Hour—a one-hour session where organization representatives and Fusion team members came together for rapid ideation around a challenge or opportunity. In this instance, the center wanted to become more well known in the community. What started with an hour-long brand sprint, transformed into a new logo and continued conversations around brand evolution. This then merged into a project around awareness, where we worked with the center to design window decals that alert community members to the center's presence and offerings in our shared community. This long-term engagement shows the Conscious Connections Model in action, aligning:

- Community needs (knowledge sharing, community, wellness) with team passions (learning, collaboration, health care).
- Team passions with organizational mission (collaboration, innovation, equity).
- Desired project outcomes (visibility and awareness) with teammate's skills (creative thinking, branding, design).

Together, Fusion and the center have increased awareness of and engagement with a needed community resource, building community and connection.

Social Responsibility in Your World

This chapter has focused on methods and tactics. The reality is that giving is a way of life. We all have an innate desire to support and help each other and to make our communities a better place to live, work, and play. Embrace this desire in your everyday. Make it a goal to positively and meaningfully impact your ecosystem and to use your passions and skills for good. Giving does not need to be a grand gesture. It can be as simple as doing a good deed for a neighbor, sharing kind words, or helping a coworker.

Teams can be intentional about building a giving culture. We have talked throughout this book about building strong teams. Give coworkers

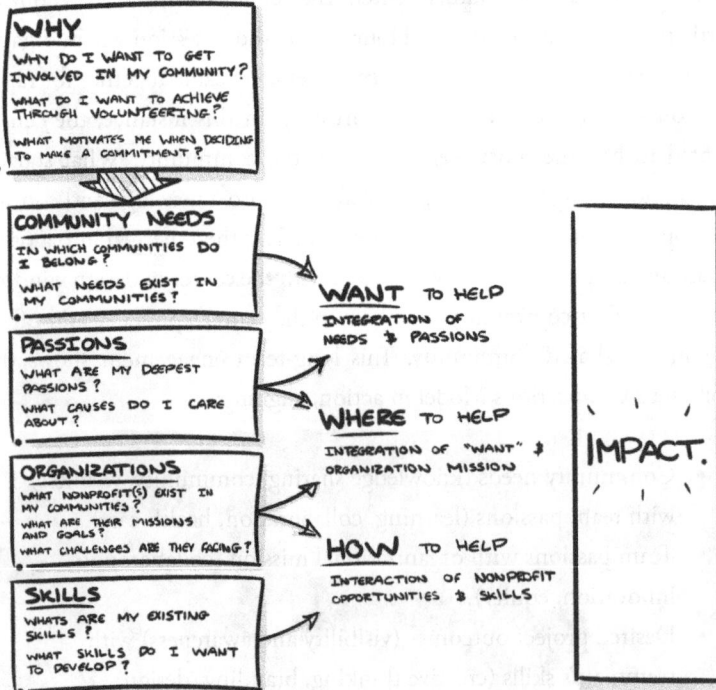

Figure 15.2 Conscious Connections model in action

the space to get to know each other as people. Practice empathy and kindness always. As a leader, build *giving* into your business model. Think about what your team can do to regularly and positively impact your ecosystem. The more you build conscious connections within your team and ecosystem, the more your team will achieve.

Take Action

You are now armed with the process to put the Conscious Connections Model (Figure 15.2) into action. It is time for your team to commit to becoming a positive force in your community and to bring impactful change to the ecosystems that you touch. Below are your immediate next steps:

Practice Empathy

Practice empathy through deeply understanding the nonprofit mindset and your team's willingness and ability to share time and skills.

- Take time to reflect on the nonprofit experience, including why organizations require volunteers and the types of relationships organizations hope to build.
- Assess team capacity and interest in volunteer work through calendar review and dedicated conversations.
- Utilize information learned to determine whether you are able to commit to volunteer work at this time. Don't worry if the answer is no; you can always reassess.

Grow Your Ecosystem

Utilize the conscious connections model to determine how your team can drive impact and build your ecosystem.

- Schedule a team meeting (at least an hour long) to complete the Conscious Connection Model, following the instructions below.

- Reach out to nonprofits of interest, identified by your team through the Conscious Connections Model, to gauge their need for support and to offer your skills.

Build a Culture of Giving

Integrate giving into your day-to-day conversations and work.

- Set regular meetings to celebrate completed volunteer work, discuss current and upcoming projects, and set new giving goals.
- Encourage and acknowledge acts of kindness and support across your ecosystem.

CHAPTER 16

Outrageous Leadership

By Edward Boudrot

One of my company's executives and I were wrapping up a Zoom meeting with leaders of a Fortune 10 company, and they were grinning from ear to ear. We'd just presented them with a program to identify, train, and empower the best talent in the world. The minute the meeting ended, my leader called me and asked, "Seven years ago, did you think we'd be on a call like that?"

Seven years ago, such a call was hard to imagine. But that was before we built a team called Fusion. Its mission was to accelerate ideas, products, and people to accelerate the growth of the enterprise. Over the years, Fusion has transformed conventional team management thinking into radical team leadership.

> Be an outrageous leader! Create a "boundless" team that breaks free from conventional confines. Invest heavily in each team member, help them create a vision for themselves, unleash their potential, accelerate their growth, transform them into exceptional leaders and you'll deliver massive value to your people and your entire enterprise.

By finding incredible talent, creating a people-centric working environment, and developing systems of personal and professional growth, Fusion has evolved into one of the highest-performing teams in our enterprise and one of the most elite consulting teams in a Fortune 10 company.

This chapter will give you the mindset and tools to be an outrageous leader and build a boundless team (Figure 16.1). Whether you're launching your career or you're a seasoned leader, you'll shift your thinking and beliefs about high-performance teams.

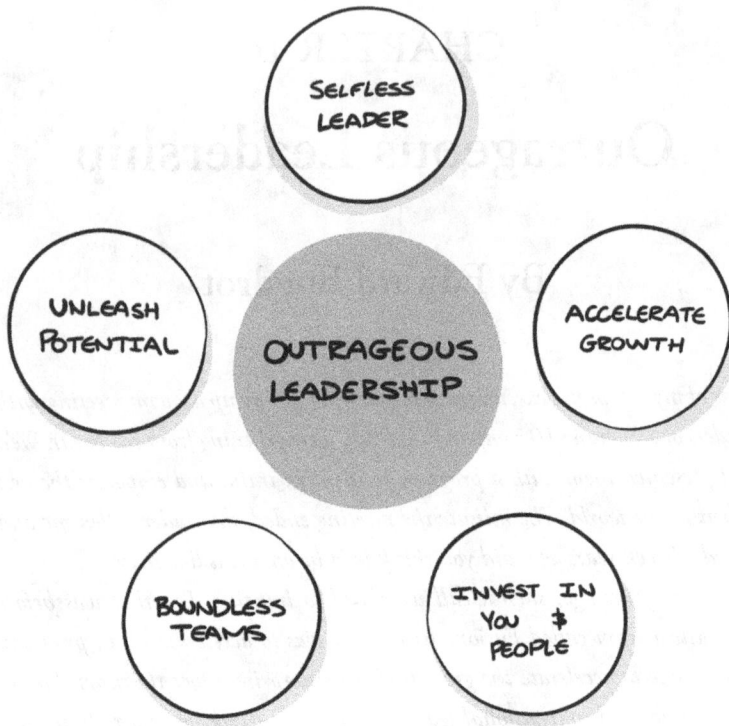

Figure 16.1 Outrageous leadership

Be a Selfless Leader: Put People First

I've learned that people will forget what you said, people will forget what you did, but people will never forget how you made them feel.[1,2]

—Maya Angelou, with original attribution to Carl W. Buehner

This quote speaks to me like no other. Truly words to live—and lead—by. Unfortunately, organizational leaders tend to focus more on output and outcomes; less on emotional connections to their team, their organization, and those they serve. Selfless leadership shifts the focus from what people deliver to who they are and how we relate to them. This people-first emphasis boosts output and outcomes (Figure 16.2). The selfless leader is deeply and genuinely committed to people:

I Care About You

Selfless leaders have people's best interests at heart. They care about the organization's mission, their team, and then themselves. They align their people with the mission's greatest good, creating purpose and igniting passion. They provide feedback that's meaningful and frequent, and they express sincere gratitude. They look for growth paths for their team members inside—and even outside of—the organization.

I Hear You, and I Want You to Feel Safe in This Environment

A selfless leader creates a positive, human-centric environment in which all voices are encouraged to speak, and all are heard. This inclusive space fosters diversity, respect, and true listening. It enables people to feel psychologically safe and supported, giving them the confidence to spread

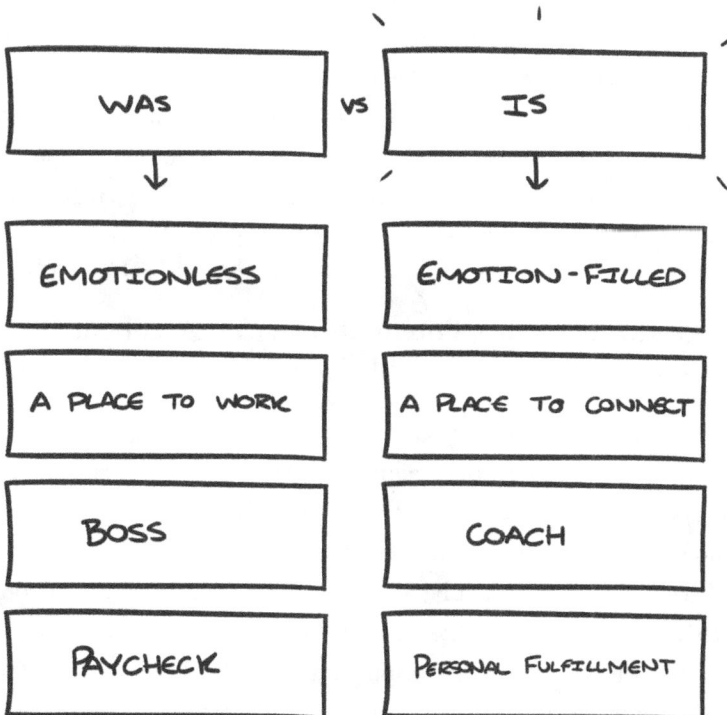

WAS	VS	IS
EMOTIONLESS		EMOTION-FILLED
A PLACE TO WORK		A PLACE TO CONNECT
BOSS		COACH
PAYCHECK		PERSONAL FULFILLMENT

Figure 16.2 People first

their wings—to strengthen their voice, commit to their own growth, expand their capabilities, and be and give their highest selves. This environment fosters deep trust, loyalty, and connection.

Take Care of Yourself, Then You Can Take Care of Your Family, and Then You Can Take Care of Work

This is a mantra I repeat often to ground my team in what's most important. When people need time off, we call upon this guiding principle. Our physical workspace is comfortable and ergonomic, and we cap the work week with a fun team activity. By demonstrating a commitment to people and their families, we further strengthen team bonds.

I'll Help You Grow (a.k.a. "360-Degree Value")

Financial compensation is important to all of us, but it's only one aspect of fulfillment. We may also feel gratified/expanded/actualized by learning, having new experiences, meeting challenges, being creative, or giving back to the world, for example. Selfless leaders seek to understand what's important to each team member. They create multiple dimensions of fulfillment—what I call "360-degree value." They access a range of resources to unleash people's gifts, bring purpose to their work, and help them grow to their full potential. The next section explains how.

Unleash People's Potential: Develop Accelerated Growth Paths

Leaders often default to conventional, structured thinking about their organization and people. But traditional talent management and leadership systems typically don't consider individuals' desires or values—never mind empower people to fulfill themselves (Figure 16.3).

That's why we devised a better, more human-centric system. It considers each team member's baseline starting point and their desired end point; then it lays a track from Point A to Point B, all the way to Point Z. In other words, it creates an accelerated (and practical) growth path.

WAS	vs	IS

TALENT MANAGEMENT SYSTEM	HUMAN POTENTIAL SYSTEM
DEFINE JOB ROLE	FREE RANGE VALUE CREATION
CAREER GROWTH	LIFE GROWTH
MANAGER	UNLEASHER

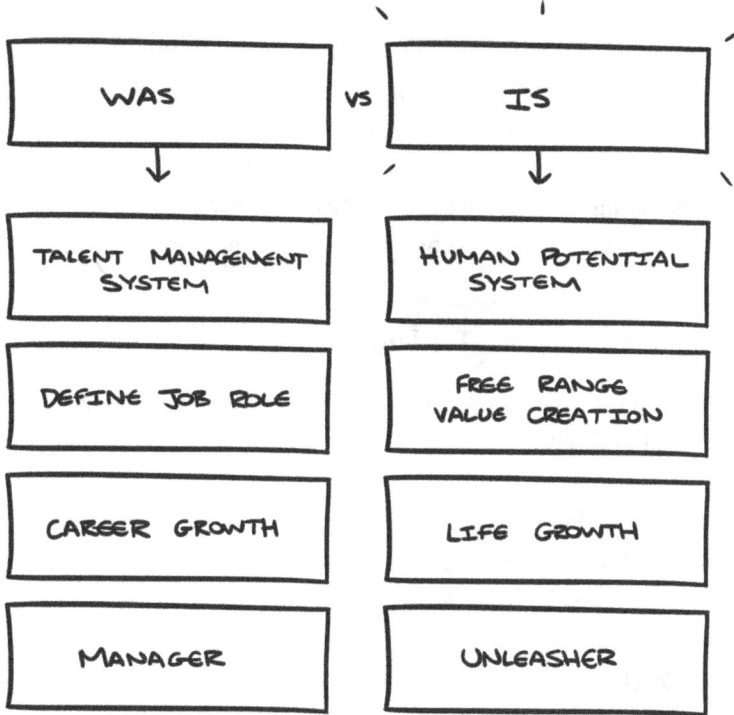

Figure 16.3 Accelerate the growth

Whether you're a team leader or a team member, you can use the following questions to plot an accelerated growth path for others or for yourself:

What Drives You?

Deeply understanding what drives you helps align motivations and personal and professional goals.

- What is important to you?
- What do you love?
- How do you want to feel?
- What are your personal aspirations?

What Impact Have You Had?

Think of impact as the contributions you've made to others, both personally and professionally. Recognizing your impact can inspire and embolden you to keep making a difference.

- What impact have you had on the enterprise?
- What impact have you had on the rest of the world?

Continual Learning and Teaching?

Think of all the experiences that have helped you develop and grow. Feel free to add to this list.

- Formal education
- Training programs
- Internships
- Work experience
- Coaching
- Mentoring
- Reading
- Webinars/Seminars
- Continuing education
- Volunteer experience
- Personal development

Where Are You Now? Where Do You Want to Be? What Would Excite You?

Reflect on your current hard and soft skills (capabilities), both within and outside of your functional area, as well as your desired capabilities (Figure 16.4).

What's Your Accelerated Growth Path?

Reflect on your Capabilities Map from the previous section and create a plan to advance from your current capabilities to your desired capabilities

```
┌─────────────────────┐     ┌─────────────────────┐
│      CURRENT        │     │  DESIRED  FUTURE    │
│   CAPABILITIES      │     │   CAPABILITIES      │
└─────────────────────┘     └─────────────────────┘
```

Figure 16.4 Capabilities map

(Figure 16.5). Consider a mix of traditional and nontraditional resources. Feel free to add to this list.

- Reading
- Webinars/Seminars
- Coaching
- Mentoring
- Continuing education
- Volunteering
- Formal education
- Training programs
- Internships
- Personal development

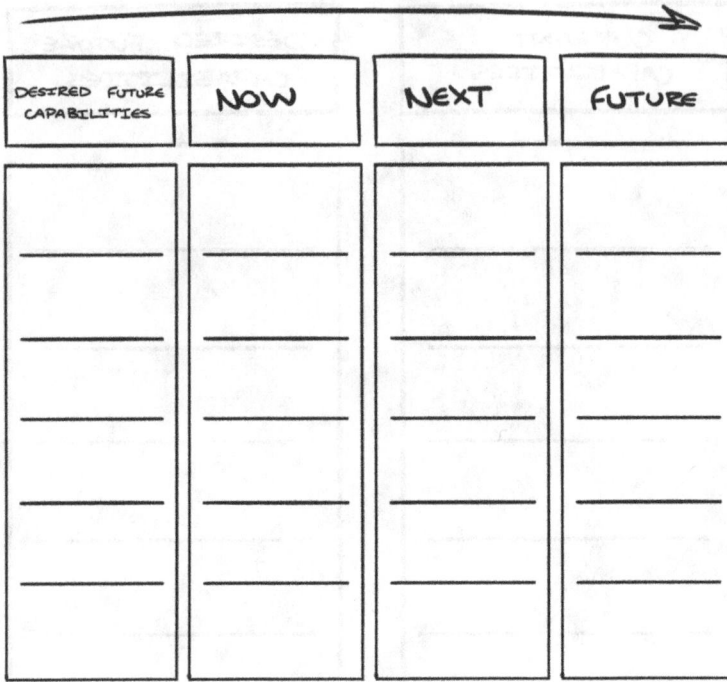

Figure 16.5 Accelerated growth path

Build a Boundless Team: Invest in Career-Making Skills

Expansion Map

When asked "Where do you want to be?" many of the Fusion team members said they want to be high-end consultants inside and outside of the enterprise. We helped them unleash their full potential and reach their goal by creating an expansion map.

After giving people guidance and feedback around the expansion map, Fusion rapidly evolved into one of the highest-performing teams in our enterprise and one of the most elite consulting teams in a Fortune 10 company. That's why we believe passionately in expansion mapping, and why I believe this approach can bring the very best out of each individual and help your team self-actualize, too.

An expansion map evaluates team members' and leaders' current capabilities. Assessing mastery level is vital: It reveals areas of potential/

COMMUNICATION	○ PRESENTING ○ CONNECT TO AUDIENCE ○ STORY ARCING ○ LEADERSHIP LANGUAGE	
TEAMING	○ LEADING ○ COACHING ○ MENTORING	FOR EACH CAPABILITY, ASSESS LEVEL OF MASTERY:
LEADERSHIP	○ SETTING VISION & DIRECTION ○ CREATING TRUST ○ INFLUENCING	1. NOVICE 2. INTERMEDIATE
SYSTEMS THINKING	○ SYNTHESIZING ○ CREATING MENTAL MODELS ○ IDEATING & PROBLEM SOLVING	3. ADVANCED 4. MASTER
DESIGN THINKING	○ HAVING EMPATHY ○ CONDUCTING USER RESEARCH ○ CONDUCTING MARKET RESEARCH ○ EXPERIMENTING	

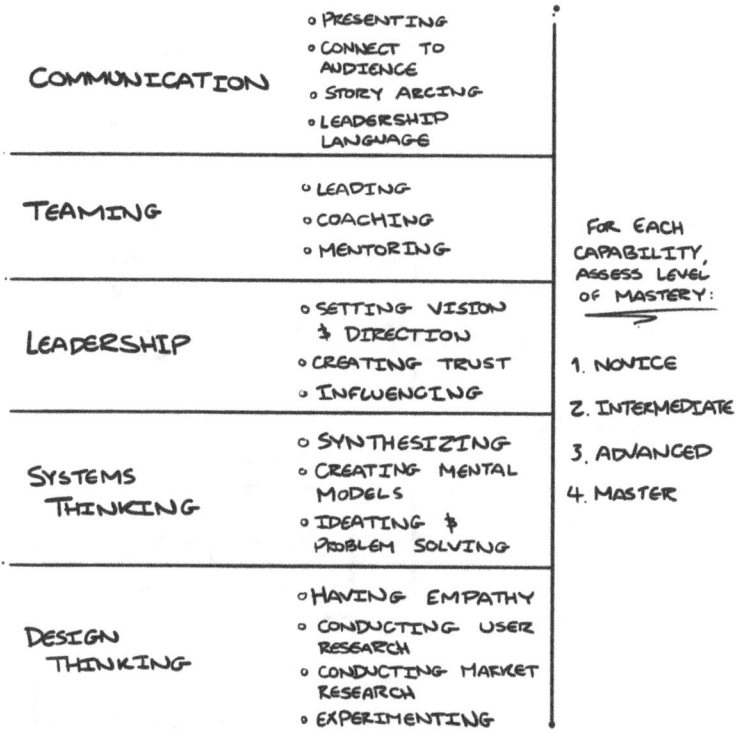

Figure 16.6 Expansion map

needed growth (Figure 16.6). The map paves the way for coaching and other strategies to raise the individual and team capabilities outlined in the Accelerated Growth path in section 5. It also holds people accountable for their growth and can be presented to new hires in order to keep the entire team running at peak performance.

Our team's expansion map focuses on capabilities that are rarely evaluated and coached, such as communication, teaming, leadership, systems thinking, and design thinking. It has created deep expertise that has accelerated individuals, the team, and the enterprise. We have developed skills that will last a lifetime and can also be leveraged outside the company.

Communication

Too often, presenters are focused on filling their allotted time. They meander without structure, recite lists of bullet points, and lose their audience.

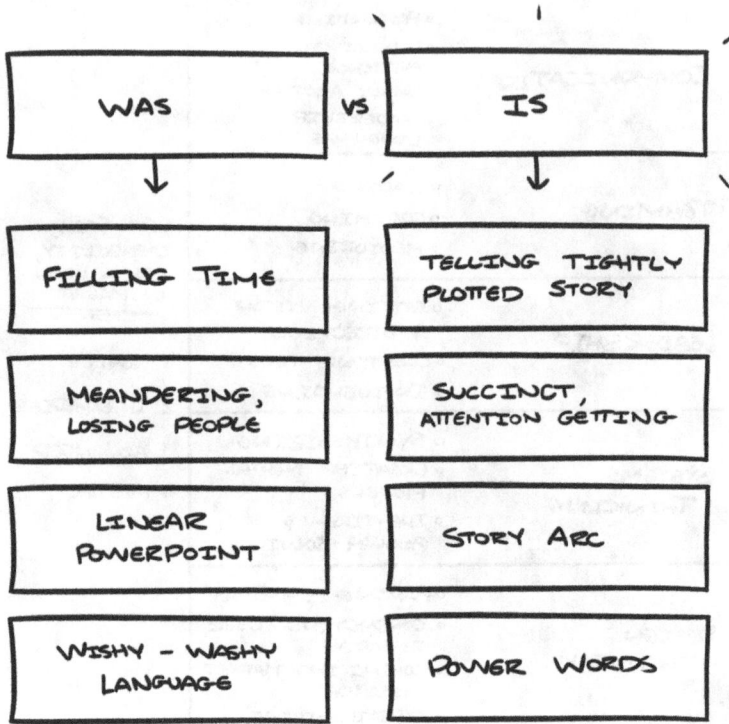

Figure 16.7 Communication

Then, there are presenters who pull in their audience and don't let them go—people you want to listen to. They have powerful stories to tell, and they tell them passionately and engagingly. These presenters rely on story arcing: they take their audience on a memorable, often emotional, journey with ups and downs. Just as effective leaders connect with their people, effective leaders connect with their audience (Figure 16.7). Here's how you can, too:

1. "Bookend" your presentation: start with a powerful story, but don't finish it.
2. State your point of view or premise.
3. Tell the audience what you want them to do.
4. Explain the benefits they'll reap.
5. Present three key points.
6. Place the other bookend: finish your story.

Teaming

"Am I a leader?" I'm often asked this question by early-career people.

No matter their title, rank, or role, my answer is always emphatic and always the same: "Yes, you are."

In a teaming culture, anyone can step up as a leader, whether within a discipline or specific to a certain situation (Figure 16.8). As a team leader, it's your job to find opportunities for people to step up. Give them the space, the floor, the spotlight, or that seat at the table in order to stretch and grow.

On our team is an early-career behavioral scientist with a passion for mindfulness. By encouraging her to create a mindfulness program for the team, we not only created a leadership opportunity for a team member but also modeled to the enterprise how personal passions can benefit the workplace.

Providing mentoring and coaching is an incredible way to help team members grow in their careers. An environment that encourages leading, following, mentoring, and coaching—independent of position—builds a high-performing team.

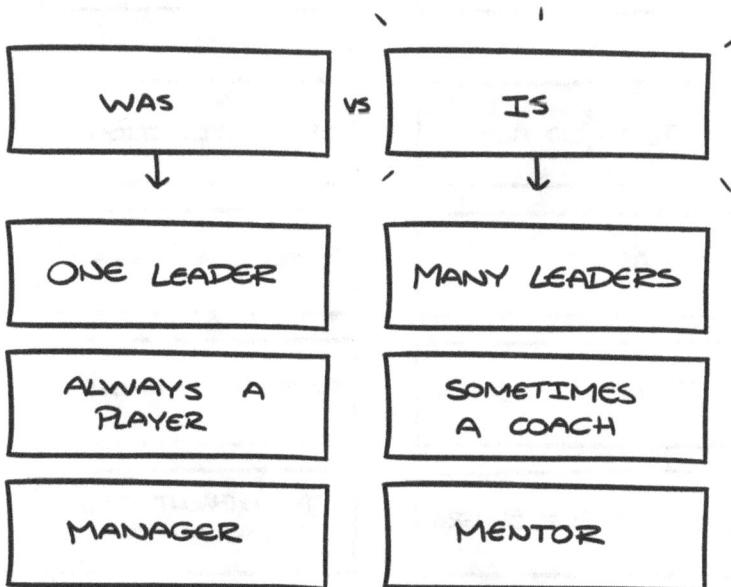

Figure 16.8 Teaming

Leadership

Leadership is about producing the next generation of leaders. My personal mantra has always been: "I'm going to be in your face, teaching you everything I know, until you can lead on your own." It's a powerful method of transferring leadership skills to others and then calling upon their leadership skills to teach you (Figure 16.9). This creates connection and trust between you and your team.

Another mark of leadership is the ability to influence others without having formal authority. Understanding your organization—up, down, and across—enables you to connect the dots between your people's capabilities and your organization's needs. Then you can determine where and how each team member can lead, and create value, within the organization. When others see your people's conviction and purity of belief, the hierarchical barriers will come tumbling down and their worth will shine through. And you'll have created massive value for your people.

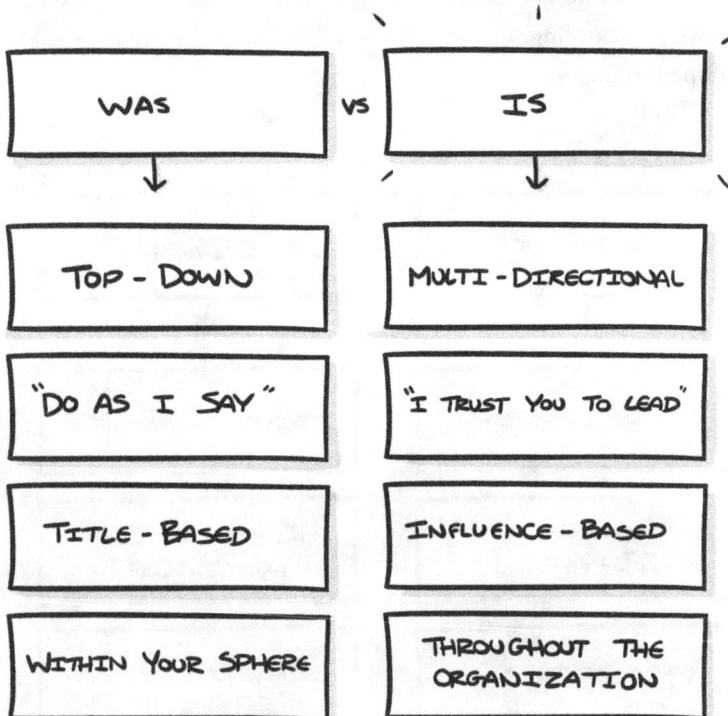

Figure 16.9 Leadership

Systems Thinking

Have you ever met that person who ties together seemingly unrelated concepts and has a massively unconventional view that somehow makes sense? They're a systems thinker. A systems thinker is constantly pulling out different frameworks, structures, and mental models to change the way people think—and change outcomes (Figure 16.10).

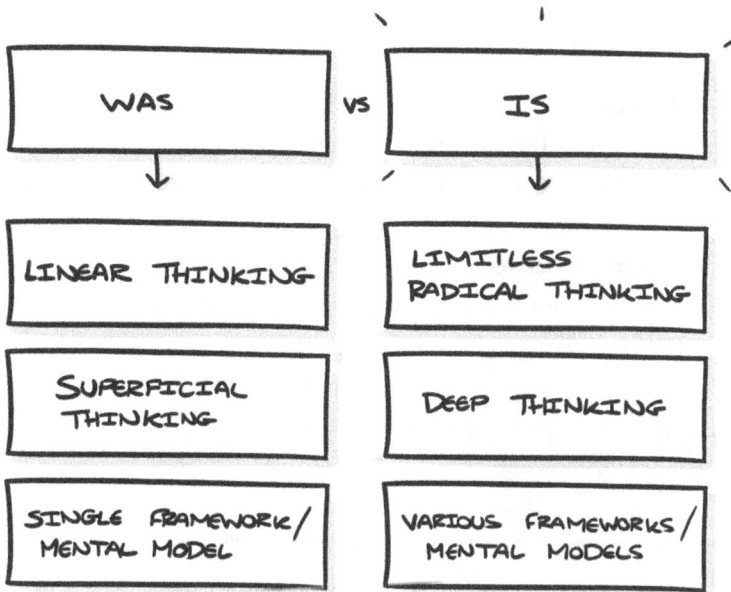

Figure 16.10 Systems thinking

You've probably heard the saying "Insanity is doing the same thing over and over again and expecting different results." Most of us default to a single mental model (think of a car stuck in gear), which can stifle our creativity and limit our effectiveness. Shifting your brain into systems-thinking gear can provide new insights and solutions.

How can you Become a Systems Thinker?

Become a polymath by reading, listening, and creating connections. But don't just read a book and recommend it to others. Take the next step: Apply your new knowledge in a structured way. Systems thinking requires time and focus. Block your calendar, remove distractions, get into a zone, and do a deep mental dive. Break down the book's framework or mental model. Apply it as an experiment and measure the results. That's the only way to drive desired outcomes.

Endless meetings, full calendars, and wasted energy—the status quo in many organizations—are the enemies of systems thinking. Are you the maverick who can say "no" to the status quo?

Design Thinking

Whether you're a CEO, product manager, or name-the-role, there is nothing more powerful than talking to those you serve. This simple step enables you to understand their needs and desires, develop empathy, and create a true emotional connection (Figure 16.11). Then, you can conduct deep market research and subject matter expert interviews to augment your foundational understanding—and learn how to develop solutions that *truly* serve those you serve.

The next step is to start experimenting with products and services as quickly as possible via pretotyping, concept testing, and rapid paper

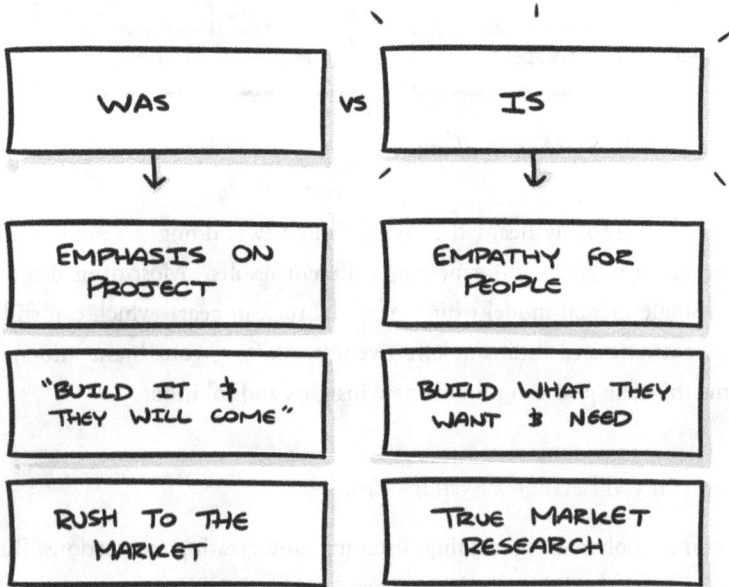

Figure 16.11 Design thinking

prototyping. These processes enable you to test your thinking at a low cost. Teaching design methodology across your team fosters a progressive mindset that always places people first.

Being an outrageous leader—creating a boundless team—brings massive value to your enterprise, your people, and those you serve.

> **Reflect:** How might you become an outrageous leader that people love? How might you inspire people and make them feel heard, seen, and valued?

Key Takeaways

Practice Selfless Leadership

Be a selfless leader, put your people first, and create a culture of connection and personal fulfillment. Ask the people around you what they love.

Unleash Potential

Unleash people's greatest potential and help them expand beyond their wildest dreams. Help your people build their Now, Next, and Future roadmap.

Build Skills

Go beyond a career plan and help people build skills that will accelerate their growth. See people's greatest gifts and help amplify them.

Be Outrageous

Be the outrageous leader who creates boundless people and teams. Create your outrageous leader plan.

Deeply Invest

Invest heavily in yourself and others in order to grow, transform, and create exceptional leaders. Create the time and space to create your investment plan and the plan for others.

Notes

Chapter 1

1. Merriam Webster (2022).
2. Harvard Business Review (2022).
3. Ibid.
4. Omah and Obiekwe (2019), pp. 23432403.
5. Decker (2009).
6. Sinek (2022).

Chapter 2

1. Stabile (2018).
2. Chestnut (2013).

Chapter 3

1. The Impact of Equality and Values on Business (2017).
2. Why Women Don't Apply For Jobs Unless They're 100% Qualified (2014).
3. Applied (2022).
4. Don't Underestimate The Importance Of Effective Onboarding (2017).
5. Bauer (2011).
6. Brown (2014).
7. Bourke and Titus (2020).
8. Bortini, Paci, Rise, and Rojnik (2017).

Chapter 4

1. TalentTelligent (2020).
2. Dweck (2017).
3. Popova (2021).
4. Blake, Crawford, Bodman, Tempany, Business Chicks, and Champ (2020).
5. Willink (2018).
6. Glassett (2019).
7. Dalio (2017).

8. The Mind Tools Content Team and Jobiero (2022).

9. World Leaders in Research-Based User Experience (2022).

10. Fogg (2020).

11. Gelb, Xiaoye, Xiaoye, Xiao, and Shanben (n.d.).

12. IMDb (2022).

13. Antoine de (1948).

14. Senge (2006).

15. O'Hagan and Lichtenberg (2020).

Chapter 5

1. Hess (2020).

2. Gladwell (2008), pp. 3567.

3. Afianian (2019).

4. Markowsky (2017).

5. Kahneman (2011), p. 35.

6. Dweck (2007).

7. Weinberg and McCann (2019), p. 113.

8. Shrestha (2017).

9. Decker (2009).

10. Kwik (2020).

11. Newport (2016).

12. Adler (1940).

13. Roediger (2014).

14. Ibid.

15. de Geus (2014).

Chapter 6

1. N.K. Jemisin's Master Class in World Building | the Ezra Klein Show (2018).

2. Home (2019).

3. Take Smart Notes (2022).

4. McPhee (2015).

5. Grant (2021).

Chapter 7

1. Editorial Team (2020).

2. Moore (2019).

3. Halo (2020).

4. Decker (2009).

Chapter 10

1. Lincoln (2019).
2. Golden State Warriors Franchise Index (2021).
3. Lee, Tian, and Willis (2018).
4. Martin (2017).
5. Van Buren and Safferstone (2009).
6. Willink (2017).
7. Helen Keller Quotes (2021).

Chapter 11

1. Maurer (2015).
2. Hogan (2015).
3. The True Cost of a Bad Hire (2015), p. 12.
4. Deckers and Decker (2015).
5. Heath and Heath (2019).
6. Klinghoffer, Young, and Haspas (2019).
7. www.urbanbound.com/blog/onboarding-infographic-statistics
8. West (2021).
9. Kurter (2018).

Chapter 12

1. Gates (2008).
2. Library of Congress (2020).
3. Reichheld, Darnell, and Burns (2021).

Chapter 13

1. Patagonia (2022).
2. Good Marketing Makes the Customer Feel Smart (2022).
3. The Quest for More Creative, Ambitious Marketing—Read the Webchat Again (2016).

Chapter 14

1. Wohlleben (2016).
2. McGilchrist (2010).
3. Wallace (2009).

4. Scott (2017).

5. Christenson (2022).

6. equityXdesign (2022).

7. United Nations Food and Agriculture Organization (2022).

Chapter 16

1. Booth and Hachiya (2004), p. 14.

2. Evans (1971), p. 244.

Bibliography

Chapter 1

Decker, B. 2009. "Feedback in Threes: Keepers, Improvements." Decker. https://decker.com/blog/feedback-in-threes-keepers-improvements-video/ (accessed January 7, 2022).

Harvard Business Review. n.d. *9 Out of 10 People Are Willing to Earn Less Money to Do More-Meaningful Work.* https://hbr.org/2018/11/9-out-of-10-people-are-willing-to-earn-less-money-to-do-more-meaningful-work (accessed January 26, 2022).

Ibid.

Merriam Webster. n.d. *Virtuous Cycle Definition and Meaning.* www.merriam-webster.com/dictionary/virtuous%20circle (accessed January 26, 2022).

Omah, O. and O. Obiekwe. 2019. "Impact of Employee Job Satisfaction on Organizational Performance." *International Journey of Current Research* 6, no. 12, pp. 23432403. www.researchgate.net/publication/338805548_Impact_of_Employee_Job_Satisfaction_on_Organizational_Performance.

Sinek, S. n.d. "How Great Leaders Inspire Action." TedTalk. www.ted.com/talks/simon_sinek_how_great_leaders_inspire_action?language=en (accessed January 26, 2022).

Chapter 2

Chestnut, B. 2013. *The Complete Enneagram: 27 Paths to Greater Self-Knowledge.* California, CA: She Writes Press, Berkeley.

Chestnut, B. 2017. *The 9 Types of Leadership: Mastering the Art of People in the 21st Century Workplace.* New York, NY: Post Hill Press.

Crystal. n.d. www.crystalknows.com/enneagram.

Heuertz, C.L. 2017. *The Sacred Enneagram: Finding Your Unique Path to Spiritual Growth.* Michigan, MI: Zondervan, Grand Rapids.

Stabile, S. 2018. *The Path Between Us: An Enneagram Journey to Healthy Relationships.* Illinois, IL: InterVarsity Press, Downers Grove.

The Enneagram Institute. n.d. www.enneagraminstitute.com/.

Chapter 3

"Applied." n.d. Beapplied.Com. www.beapplied.com/ (accessed January 4, 2022).

"Don't Underestimate The Importance Of Effective Onboarding." August 10, 2017. Shrm.Org. www.shrm.org/resourcesandtools/hr-topics/talent-acquisition/pages/doesn't-underestimate-the-importance-of-effective-onboarding.aspx.

"The Impact of Equality and Values on Business." 2017. Salesforce.Com. www.salesforce.com/contents/impact-of-equality/.

"Why Women Don't Apply For Jobs Unless They're 100% Qualified." 2014. https://hbr.org/2014/08/why-women-dont-apply-for-jobs-unless-theyre-100-qualified.

Bauer, T.N. 2011. *Onboarding New Employees: Maximizing Success.* www.shrm.org/foundation/ourwork/initiatives/resources-from-past-initiatives/documents/onboarding%20new%20employees.pdf.

Bortini, P., A. Paci, A. Rise, and I. Rojnik. 2017. *Inclusive Leadership: Theoretical Framework.* https://inclusiveleadership.eu/il_theoreticalframework_en.pdf.

Bourke, J. and A. Titus. 2020. *The Key to Inclusive Leadership.* https://hbr.org/2020/03/the-key-to-inclusive-leadership.

Brown, B. 2014. *The Gifts of Imperfection.* Tsai Fong Books.

Chapter 4

Blake, G., D. Crawford, R. Bodman, A. Tempany, Business Chicks, and N. Champ. August 25, 2020. *17 Badass Brené Brown Quotes That Will Inspire You to Lead.* Business Chicks. https://businesschicks.com/brene-brown-quotes/.

Dalio, R. 2017. *Principles.* Simon and Schuster.

Dweck, C. 2017. *Mindset.* London: Robinson.

Fogg, B.J. 2020. *Tiny Habits: The Small Changes That Change Everything.* Waterville, Maine, ME: Thorndike Press.

Gelb, David, E. Xiaoye, Z. Xiaoye, Y. Xiao, and Y. Shanben. n.d. *Shou Si Zhi Shen Jiro Dreams of Sushi.*

IMDb. n.d. "Jiro Dreams of Sushi." IMDb.com. www.imdb.com/title/tt1772925/characters/nm4807635 (accessed January 24, 2022).

Nick Glassett. October 9, 2019. *Jocko Willink 'Good' Transcript: Origin Leadership Group.* https://nickglassett.com/jocko-willink-good-transcript/.

Nielsen Norman Group. n.d. "Design Thinking 101." World Leaders in Research-Based User Experience. www.nngroup.com/articles/design-thinking/ (accessed January 24, 2022).

Popova, M. August 31, 2021. "Fixed Vs. Growth: The Two Basic Mindsets That Shape Our Lives." *The Marginalian.* www.themarginalian.org/2014/01/29/carol-dweck-mindset/.

Saint-Exupéry, A. 1948. *Citadelle*. Gallimard.

Senge, P.M. 2006. *The Fifth Discipline*. London: Random House Business.

TalentTelligent, LLC. 2020. *Common Language of Leadership: Leader Behavior Library*. UnitedHealth Group. https://uhgazure.sharepoint.com/sites/cll/Shared%20Documents/Forms/AllItems.aspx?id=%2Fsites%2Fcll%2FShared%20Documents%2FCLL%20Central%20Folders%2FCLL%2DLeader%2DInteractive%2DLibrary%2Epdf&parent=%2Fsites%2Fcll%2FShared%20Documents%2FCLL%20Central%20Folders.

The Mind Tools Content Team and Jobiero. n.d. "OGSM Frameworks: Making Your Strategy a Reality." Strategy Skills Training From MindTools.com. www.mindtools.com/pages/article/ogsm-frameworks.htm (accessed January 24, 2022).

Willink, J. 2018. *Extreme Ownership*. S.l.: Pan Macmillan Australia.

Chapter 5

Adler, M. 1940. *How to Read a Book*. New York, NY: Simon & Schuster.

Afianian, A. 2019. "What Separates Elite Achievers From Average Performers?" *Medium*. https://forge.medium.com/what-separates-elite-performers-from-the-average-the-berlin-study-c1d00698c030 (accessed 7 January 2022).

Cirollo, F. n.d. "The Pomodoro Technique." *Cirillo Consulting*. https://francescocirillo.com/pages/pomodoro-technique (accessed 7 January 2022).

de Geus, A. August 1, 2014. "Planning as Learning." *Harvard Business Review*. https://hbr.org/1988/03/planning-as-learning.

Decker, B. 2009. "Feedback in Threes: Keepers, Improvements." *Decker*. https://decker.com/blog/feedback-in-threes-keepers-improvements-video/ (accessed 7 January 2022).

Dweck, C. 2007. *Mindset: The New Psychology of Success*. New York, NY: Penguin Random House.

Gladwell, M. 2008. *Outliers: The Story of Success*. New York, NY: Little, Brown and Company.

Hess, ed. 2020. *Hyper-learning: How to Adapt to the Speed of Change*. California, CA: Berrett-Koehler Publishers.

Kahneman, D. 2011. *Thinking, Fast and Slow*. New York, NY: Farrar, Straus and Giroux.

Kwik, J. 2020. "Activating Learning Mindset With Simon Sinek." *Kwik Brain With Jim Kwik Podcast Episode 168*. https://jimkwik.com/kwik-brain-episode168-activating-learning-mindset-with-simon-sinek/ (accessed 7 January 2022).

Markowsky, G. 2017. "Information Theory" *Encyclopedia Britannica*. www.britannica.com/science/information-theory (accessed 7 January 2022).

Newport, C. 2016. *Deep Work: Rules for Focused Success in a Distracted World.* New York, NY: Grand Central Publishing.

Roediger , H.L., M.A. McDaniel, P. Brown. 2014. *Make it Stick: The Science of Successful Learning.* Cambridge, Massachusetts, MA: Harvard University Press.

Shrestha, P. 2017. "Ebbinghaus Forgetting Curve." *Psychestudy.* www.psychestudy. com/cognitive/memory/ebbinghaus-forgetting-curve (accessed 7 January 2022).

Weinberg, G. and L. McCann. 2019. *Super Thinking: The Big Book of Mental Models.* New York, NY: Penguin Random House.

Chapter 6

"N.K. Jemisin's Master Class in World Building | the Ezra Klein Show." August 27, 2018. YouTube. www.youtube.com/watch?v=I6xyFQhbsjQ.

McPhee, J. September 7, 2015. "The Art of Omission." *The New Yorker.* www. newyorker.com/magazine/2015/09/14/omission.

"Home." June 22, 2019. Getting Things Done®. https://gettingthingsdone.com/.

BrandSanderson. January 22, 2020. *Lecture #1: Introduction—Brandon Sanderson on Writing Science Fiction and Fantasy.* YouTube. www.youtube.com/ watch?v=-6HodHEeosc.

Grant, A. January 3, 2021. *Originals.* www.adamgrant.net/book/originals/.

"Write ... One Note at a Time." January 31, 2022. Take Smart Notes. https:// takesmartnotes.com/ (accessed January 31, 2022).

Chapter 7

Ben, D. 2009. *Feedback in Threes: Keepers, Improvements.* Decker https://decker. com/blog/feedback-in-threes-keepers-improvements-video/ (accessed 7 January 2022).

Editorial Team. 2020. *21 Collaboration Statistics that Show the Power of Teamwork!.* https://blog.bit.ai/collaboration-statistics/ (accessed December 28, 2021).

Halo. 2020. *10 Amazing Statistics to Celebrate National Gratitude Month.* https://halo.com/10-amazing-statistics-to-celebrate-national-gratitude-month/#:~:text=In%20a%20study%20of%20800,well%2Dbeing%20 by%2010%25 (accessed December 28, 2021).

Kaleigh, M. 2019. *Workplace Accountability Done Right.* https://Monday.com/ blog/teamwork/workplace-accountability/ (accessed November 11, 2021).

Chapter 10

"Golden State Warriors Franchise Index." n.d. Basketball. www.basketball-reference.com/teams/GSW/ (accessed December 14, 2021).

BrainyQuote.com. 2021. "Vincent Van Gogh Quotes." *BrainyMedia Inc.* www.brainyquote.com/quotes/vincent_van_gogh_120866. (accessed December 14, 2021).

"Pat Summitt Quotes." n.d. Quotefancy. https://quotefancy.com/pat-summitt-quotes (accessed January 29, 2022).

BrainyQuote.com. 2021. "Helen Keller Quotes." BrainyMedia Inc. www.brainyquote.com/quotes/helen_keller_382259 (accessed December 14, 2021).

Van Buren, M.E. and T. Safferstone. January 1, 2009. "The Quick Wins Paradox." *Harvard Business Review.* https://hbr.org/2009/01/the-quick-wins-paradox.

Willink, J. February 2, 2017. "Extreme Ownership | Jocko Willink | TEDxUniversityofNevada." Educational Video, 13:49.

Martin, B. August 18, 2017. "Larry Bird: By the Numbers." *NBA Stats.* www.nba.com/stats/articles/larry-bird-by-the-numbers.

Clarabut, J. February 23, 2018. "The Strength of the Team Is Each Individual Member. The Strength of Each Member Is the Team— Phil Jackson." *Wellbeing People.* www.wellbeingpeople.com/2018/02/23/strength-team-individual-member-strength-member-team-phil-jackson/#:~:text=Information-,%E2%80%9Cthe%20strength%20of%20the%20team%20is%20each%20individual%20member.,Phil%20Jackson.

Lee, A., A.W. Tian, and S. Willis. March 2, 2018. "When Empowering Employees Works, and When It Doesn't." *Harvard Business Review.* https://hbr.org/2018/03/when-empowering-employees-works-and-when-it-doesn't.

Lincoln, J. June 6, 2019. "17 Inspirational Quotes to Instantly Foster Teamwork When Unity Is Lost." Entrepreneur." *Entrepreneur.* www.entrepreneur.com/article/269941.

Chapter 11

Ben, D. 2009. "Feedback in Threes: Keepers, Improvements." *Decker.* https://decker.com/blog/feedback-in-threes-keepers-improvements-video/ (accessed 7 January 2022).

Heath, C. and D. Heath. 2019. *The Power of Moments: Why Certain Experiences Have Extraordinary Impact.* Corgi.

Jan, W., Ph.D. 2021. "The Truth About Job Satisfaction and Friendships at Work." *National Business Research Institute.* www.nbrii.com/employee-survey-white-papers/the-truth-about-job-satisfaction-and-friendships-at-work/.

Klinghoffer, D., C. Young, and D. Haspas. June 6, 2019. "Every New Employee Needs an Onboarding 'Buddy'." *Harvard Business Review.* https://hbr.org/2019/06/every-new-employee-needs-an-onboarding-buddy.

Kurter, H.L. December 3, 2018. "10 Simple Ways to Improve Onboarding for Increased Retention." *Forbes.* www.forbes.com/sites/heidilynnekurter/2018/12/03/10-simple-ways-to-improve-onboarding-for-increased-retention/amp/.

Maren H. May 29, 2015. "How to Get Employee Onboarding Right." *Forbes.* www.forbes.com/sites/theyec/2015/05/29/how-to-get-employee-onboarding-right/#1e907590407b.

Roy M. April 16, 2015. "Onboarding Key to Retaining, Engaging Talent." SHRM. www.shrm.org/resourcesandtools/hr-topics/talent-acquisition/pages/new-employee-onboarding-guide.aspx.

Schawbel, D. November 2018. "Why Work Friendships Are Critical for Long-Term Happiness." CNBC. www.cnbc.com/2018/11/13/why-work-friendships-are-critical-for-long-term-happiness.html.

The True Cost of a Bad Hire. August 2015. p. 12. Brandon Hall Group. https://b2b-assets.glassdoor.com/the-true-cost-of-a-bad-hire.pdf.

Chapter 12

Bill, G. September 1, 2021. *A New Approach to Capitalism in the 21st Century.* https://news.microsoft.com/2008/01/24/bill-gates-world-economic-forum-2008.

Library of Congress. September 1, 2021. General Information. www.loc.gov/about/general-information.

Reichheld, F., D. Darnell, and M. Burns. September 1, 2021. *Net Promoter 3.0 A Better System for Understanding the Real Value of Happy Customers.* https://hbr.org/2021/11/net-promoter-3-0.

Chapter 13

Good Marketing Makes the Customer Feel Smart. n.d. Cram. www.cram.com/essay/Good-Marketing-Makes-The-Customer-Feel-Smart/FK9FQYAZ7MWW (accessed January 7, 2022).

Patagonia. n.d. *Our Business and Climate Change.* www.patagonia.com.au/pages/our-business-and-climate-change#:~:text=Patagonia's%20mission%20statement%20reads%3A%20%E2%80%9CBuild,if%20we%20hope%20to%20survive (accessed January 7, 2022).

The Guardian. April 27, 2016. "The Quest for More Creative, Ambitious Marketing—Read the Webchat Again." *Guardian News and Media.* www.theguardian.com/media-network/2016/apr/27/creative-ambitious-marketing-webchat.

Chapter 14

Christenson, C. n.d. *Theory of the Jobs To Be Done.* https://hbr.org/2005/12/marketing-malpractice-the-cause-and-the-cure (accessed January 2022).

equityXdesign. n.d. *Equity Pause.* https://dschool.stanford.edu/resources/equity-centered-design-framework (accessed in January 2022).

Frances F. n.d. *How to rebuild trust.* https://blog.ted.com/how-to-rebuild-trust-frances-frei-speaks-at-ted2018/ (accessed January 2022).

McGilchrist, I. 2010. The Master and His Emissary; The Divided Brain and the Making of the Western World. Yale University Press.

Scott, K. 2017. *Radical Candor.* New York, NY: St. Martin's Press.

United Nations Food and Agriculture Organization. n.d. https://www.bbc.com/news/science-environment-34173502 (accessed in January 2022).

Wallace, D.F. 2009. *This is Water.* Little, Brown and Company.

Wohlleben, P. 2016. *Hidden Life of Trees.* Vancouver: Greystone Books.

Chapter 15

Godfrey, J. 2013. *Raising Financially Fit Kids.* New York, NY: Ten Speed Press.

Chapter 16

David B. and M. Hachiya. 2004. *The Arts Go to School: Classroom-Based Activities That Focus on Music, Painting, Drama, Movement, Media, and More.* Quote Page 14. Published by Markham, Ontario: Pembroke Publishers. Distributed by Portland, Maine: Stenhouse Publishers.

Evans, R.L. 1971. *Richard Evans' Quote Book, ("Selected From the 'Spoken Word' and 'Thought for the Day' and From Many Inspiring Thought-Provoking Sources From Many Centuries").* Quote Page 244, Column 2. Salt Lake City, Utah: Publishers Press.

About the Authors

Poems

Lianza Reyes

Lianza is a small business owner who writes custom poetry for clients balanced with sophisticated usability studies with a focus on diverse learning, accessibility, and interaction styles. She has educational backgrounds in Broadcast and Digital Journalism, Design Thinking and Innovation, and Information Science with a focus on Human–Computer Interaction.

Chapter 1

Colby Champagne

Colby is energized by the idea of creating a lasting impact and improving the lives of those she serves. This energy, coupled with her natural inquisitiveness and constant desire to learn, is what attracts her to complex problems within healthcare. She approaches her work through a lens of empathy, compassion, and humility, operating under a personal mission to drive systemic change that creates an equitable world for all.

Chapter 2

Jeremy Smith

Jeremy has over two decades of design experience spread across print, branding, and digital experiences. For the past 8 years, he has been leading teams and designing experiences for a Fortune 10 healthcare company. His passion for investigating root causes and motivation has led him to studying all manner of user behavior and psychology. Jeremy enjoys learning from other people (whether through observation or conversation), working with his hands, and trail running in the early morning.

Chapter 3

Sarah Konstantino

Sarah is an experienced, design-driven product strategist with a demonstrated history of working in healthcare technology and services. She is passionate about using empathy and industry-proven frameworks to solve big problems and drive meaningful innovation within the healthcare industry. She also works diligently with industry leaders to identify and improve inclusion and diversity strategies in support of business growth and objectives.

Chapter 4

Ryan Tyler

Ryan Tyler is the Senior Director of Product Experience for a Fortune 10 healthcare company. Ryan is a consumer-focused advocate with over 20 years of consulting history focused on customer engagement and user-centered, interaction design. In the 9 years that he has been with his current company, he has had the opportunity to collaborate with and manage teams of highly talented designers and user experience specialists who have helped bring new processes and approaches for solving problems into the market faster.

Chapter 5

Sarah Witty

Sarah prides herself on bringing a critical eye to all she does and challenging assumptions in order to create the highest value for customers. Her curious nature has led Sarah to explore across disciplines and continents, always seeking to better understand the perspective of others. As a product experience manager at Fusion, Sarah has driven teams from good to great by coaching the foundations of Team Performance and Inclusive Culture.

Chapter 6

Jacob Colling

Jacob helps teams solve complex problems. He has shaken down product portfolios and roadmaps, helped launch product pilots in new markets, ran postmortems for product teams, and created enterprise technology strategies. Outside of work, he loves to explore the outdoors by hiking, climbing, and cycling. When not outside, he is generally reading, drinking coffee, or tinkering on some side project.

Chapter 7

Patrick Hanley

Patrick, who goes by Pat, loves helping people in need by creating products, services, and experiences with a design thinking mindset. Succeeding in both the healthcare and toy industries, he continues to push creative boundaries and redefines what "good" design means with various tools, frameworks, and processes. His secret to creating beautiful experiences is listening to his users, walking in their shoes, and figuring out what their needs are, to not only create something cool but create something they need.

Chapter 8

Haya Alzaid López

Haya has a passion for understanding human behavior, desire, and motivation. This passion has set her on an entre(intra)preneurial path where she adapts user-oriented design frameworks to translate insights from consumer research into innovative business models, products, and services. She has led countless clients toward innovative solutions in a wide range of industries including healthcare, medical devices, consumer products, social enterprises, and nonprofits. You can also find her watching Broadway Musicals with her husband or running around parks with Terabyte and Gigaflop, their very energetic, goofy, and nerdy Rottweilers.

Chapter 9

Caitlin Geissler

Caitlin is a pragmatic optimist and concept visionary compelled to change the world through enhanced experiences and mindsets. As a product and strategy leader, she combines the essentials of logic, creativity, and diplomacy in the face of constant change to help teams achieve breakthroughs. Her lifelong passion for sports, history, and culture inspires and can be found in the approach and models she brings forth in her work.

Chapter 10

Trey Bliss

Trey is a lifelong athlete and hails from a lineage of teachers and coaches. As a Computer Science and Economics graduate, he brings a practical and process-driven approach to areas generally thought of as soft skills. Trey is a believer in team before self. He believes that the best journey to success is one walking with others. By surrounding yourself with highly motivated and driven individuals you can excel in social, athletic, and corporate environments. Outside of work, Trey aims to experience everything life has to offer from competing in sports to traveling the world to sitting down with a good book.

Chapter 11

Brittany Drury

Brittany is an explorer of the human experience. Her unique insights are drawn from 14 years as a former professional athlete, coach, and international performer, combined with a formal background in process improvement and human-centered design. The result? A passion for pushing the bar and a restless quest to drive elite team performance. Her extensive cross-cultural experiences in over 80 countries ground her perspective in authentic, meaningful collaborations that inspire human connection.

Chapter 12

Shane Picciotto

Shane is a detective and engineer at heart. Shane studied mechanical engineering at MIT and has worked in product for his entire career. At work, he's part of the Fusion team. At home, he can be found fending off his cats in the kitchen while testing recipes.

He has benefited immensely from the time and wisdom of others. He welcomes the opportunity to pass that on to others through e-mail, phone call, or coffee. His goal is spreading pronoia (the idea that everyone is out to help you).

Chapter 13

Alexa Colyer

Alexa leads and influences others to achieve their goals in order to excite and engage the universe and deliver impactful outcomes. She leverages her "expertise trifecta" of technology, experience, and product strategy to engage with others, drive excitement, and guide leaders to action. Since 2020, Alexa has brought her team's marketing efforts to a new level. The content within this chapter reflects on her learnings, insights, and perspectives gained through this work.

Chapter 14

Emma Stone

Emma is a behavioral scientist/researcher/strategist/puzzler/designer/ accessibility advocate who has a neuroscience degree from Harvard. She strives to connect with people holistically, understand behavior deeply, and solve complex problems creatively. Her primary method: ask a lot of questions and get hands-on with a solution.

Chapter 15

Julie Williams

Julie Williams is a strong believer that all have the ability to positively impact their communities. Combining her 10+ years of nonprofit experience with a passion for process and a love of teaching, Julie enables others to practice servant leadership and philanthropy in their everyday lives. When not diligently collaborating with her Fusion teammates, Julie can be found exploring the outdoors or contemplating her next trip.

Chapter 16

Edward Boudrot

Ed serves as the Vice President of Fusion, harnessing his extensive background from Fortune 500 settings, including Intuit, and dynamic technology startups. He is a master in crafting experiences and product innovations, thriving on transforming abstract concepts into concrete, viable products. His approach combines a relentless "get it done" attitude with sharp skills honed at Babson College and extensive experience in emerging markets. Ed pioneered the "Fusion" concept, integrating market research, human-centered design, product management, experience management, and development into a cohesive process that rapidly delivers effective market solutions.

Index

OTHER TITLES IN THE HUMAN RESOURCE MANAGEMENT AND ORGANIZATIONAL BEHAVIOR COLLECTION

Michael Provitera, Barry University, Editor

- *The Negotiation Edge* by Michael Saksa
- *Applied Leadership* by Sam Altawil
- *Forging Dynasty Businesses* by Chuck Violand
- *How the Harvard Business School Changed the Way We View Organizations* by Jay W. Lorsch
- *Managing Millennials* by Jacqueline Cripps
- *Personal Effectiveness* by Lucia Strazzeri
- *Catalyzing Transformation* by Sandra Waddock
- *Critical Leadership and Management Tools for Contemporary Organizations* by Tony Miller
- *Leading From the Top* by Dennis M. Powell
- *Warp Speed Habits* by Marco Neves
- *I Don't Understand* by Buki Mosaku
- *Nurturing Equanimity* by Michael Edmondson
- *Speaking Up at Work* by Ryan E. Smerek
- *Living a Leadership Lifestyle* by Ross Emerson
- *Business Foresight* by Tony Grundy

Concise and Applied Business Books

The Collection listed above is one of 30 business subject collections that Business Expert Press has grown to make BEP a premiere publisher of print and digital books. Our concise and applied books are for...

- Professionals and Practitioners
- Faculty who adopt our books for courses
- Librarians who know that BEP's Digital Libraries are a unique way to offer students ebooks to download, not restricted with any digital rights management
- Executive Training Course Leaders
- Business Seminar Organizers

Business Expert Press books are for anyone who needs to dig deeper on business ideas, goals, and solutions to everyday problems. Whether one print book, one ebook, or buying a digital library of 110 ebooks, we remain the affordable and smart way to be business smart. For more information, please visit www.businessexpertpress.com, or contact sales@businessexpertpress.com.